SCHOOL STRIKE 4 CLIMATE

# BE THE CHANGE

## ROB GREENFIELD'S
## — *Call to Kids* —

## MAKING A DIFFERENCE
## *in a* MESSED-UP WORLD

### ROB GREENFIELD AND
### ANTONIA BANYARD

## GREYSTONE KIDS
GREYSTONE BOOKS • VANCOUVER/BERKELEY/LONDON

To all the family,
community, and teachers
who raised me to be a
good human. To all the
teachers dedicated to
educating and loving the
children of the world. To
all the people serving as
positive role models for
the younger generation.
To all the children and
young adults standing up
for a better world. This
book is dedicated to you.
—Love, Rob

For S and B, always,
and their generation.
And the next one.
And the one after that.
And the one after that.
—Toni

Greystone Kids / Greystone Books Ltd.
greystonebooks.com

Cataloguing data available from Library and Archives Canada
ISBN 978-1-77164-591-1 (cloth)
ISBN 978-1-77164-592-8 (epub)

Editing by Linda Pruessen
Proofreading by Alison Strobel
Indexing by Catherine Marjoribanks
Cover and interior design by Belle Wuthrich

Printed and bound in Singapore on FSC® certified paper at COS Printers Pte Ltd. The FSC® label means that materials used for the product have been responsibly sourced.

Greystone Books gratefully acknowledges the Musqueam, Squamish, and Tsleil-Waututh peoples on whose land our Vancouver head office is located.

Greystone Books thanks the Canada Council for the Arts, the British Columbia Arts Council, the Province of British Columbia through the Book Publishing Tax Credit, and the Government of Canada for supporting our publishing activities.

MIX
Paper from
responsible sources
FSC® C016973

BRITISH COLUMBIA

BRITISH COLUMBIA
ARTS COUNCIL
An agency of the Province of British Columbia

Canada Council
for the Arts

Conseil des arts
du Canada

# CONTENTS

## INTRODUCTION
2

### 1
## STUFF
4

### 2
## WASTE
12

### 3
## FOOD WASTE
20

### 4
## the FOOD SYSTEM
28

### 5
## WATER
36

### 6
## ENERGY
44

### 7
## TRANSPORTATION
52

### 8
## MONEY
60

### 9
## CONNECTION
68

## CONCLUSION
76

Glossary 78

Resources 80

Selected Sources 81

Image Credits 83

Index 85

Acknowledgments 87

About the Authors 87

# How to Be the Change You Wish to See in the World

**AS YOU READ THESE PAGES,** you'll get to know me as the guy who walked around New York City for a month, wearing all his trash; biked across the United States on a bamboo bicycle; lived off the grid in a tiny house; dove into thousands of grocery store dumpsters…and ate food from them!

I'm an activist and adventurer on a mission to inspire positive change in the world.

But I wasn't always this way.

Growing up in a small town in Wisconsin, I loved to spend every moment I could playing outside with frogs and turtles, and fishing.

When I was about eight I learned that some frogs were growing an extra pair of legs because of toxic pollution. I remember photos of birds

My mom took me and my brothers and sister camping in the summers. These experiences inspired my lifelong connection to nature.

covered in black goop from oil spills. But I didn't see how my actions at home or school were really connected to these things. I thought my life was separate from the environment. I might have even thought I was living "environmentally friendly" because my mom taught me the basics, like recycling and conserving water and electricity.

# I want to really *be* the change I wish to see in the world.

Then, when I was about 25, I realized I had to totally transform my life. I was watching documentaries and reading books and I learned that my daily actions—the food I was eating, the shiny car I was driving, the clothes I was wearing, and all the stuff I had collected—were contributing to the destruction of the environment. I was part of the reason those frogs were mutating and birds were covered in oil.

So I set out to change my life. Rather than feeling overwhelmed and scared, I made a list of positive changes I could make and then committed to making at least one every week. I started with small steps, like eating more fresh fruits and veggies instead of packaged foods, and worked up to big changes, like getting rid of my gas-guzzling car. Every time I did something that was good for the Earth, it was also good for me. With these changes, I was becoming much happier and much healthier.

I decided to become an environmental activist. And that's when all the adventures began.

I want to lead by example, but I also want to live my message out loud. I want to really *be* the change I wish to see in the world, to quote the well-known expression by Gandhi. So I embark on extreme adventures that are designed to catch the attention of people and the media. My goal isn't to get anyone to do exactly what I'm doing.

Instead, I want to inspire people to ask themselves questions about the way they're living. And if they don't like the answers, I want to empower them to change for the better. That's where you come in.

In this book, you're going to learn a lot. The first four pages of each chapter will give you information about one aspect of your life, like trash, or food, or water, or energy. That information might get you thinking. You might even feel overwhelmed. But this isn't a book of problems. It's a book of *solutions*.

The next two pages of each chapter will tell you the story of my adventures. Perhaps my journey will inspire you by demonstrating what one person can do.

The last two pages of each chapter offer ideas about what you can do, or what other people are already doing to be part of the solution. My hope is that these ideas will give you the tools to be the change *you* wish to see in the world.

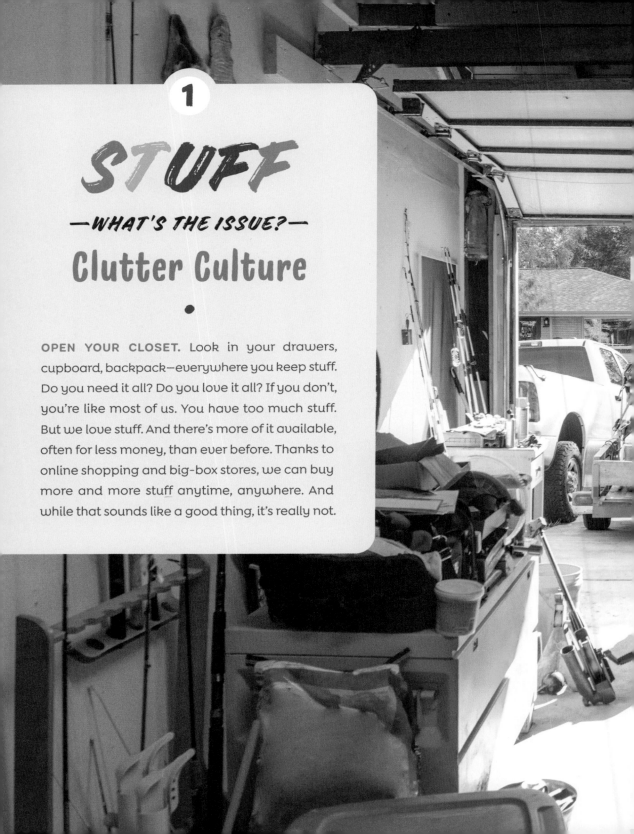

# 1

# STUFF

## —WHAT'S THE ISSUE?—

## Clutter Culture

•

**OPEN YOUR CLOSET.** Look in your drawers, cupboard, backpack—everywhere you keep stuff. Do you need it all? Do you love it all? If you don't, you're like most of us. You have too much stuff. But we love stuff. And there's more of it available, often for less money, than ever before. Thanks to online shopping and big-box stores, we can buy more and more stuff anytime, anywhere. And while that sounds like a good thing, it's really not.

## More Stuff, Bigger Houses

So how much stuff do we really have, and how much of it is necessary? On average, American children receive 70 new toys a year, and while 10-year-olds in the United Kingdom typically own more than 200 toys, they actually play with only a dozen or so.

Where do we keep all that stuff? The typical American house is about 2,500 square feet (232 m²), almost three times larger than the average house in the 1950s, even though families are smaller than they used to be.

And still, our bigger houses aren't big enough. So some people rent storage units. Since 2015, the self-storage industry has grown almost three times faster than the population has.

## The Clutter Blues

Surprisingly, all of our extra possessions are not necessarily making us happier. In 1957, just over one-third of Americans described themselves as "very happy." Since then, despite buying more every year, Americans are no happier.

Once our basic needs are comfortably met, more doesn't always mean better. You might notice that you don't love everything in your closet or on your shelves. If you had only one pair of jeans, you'd be very happy to have it, but your 50th pair won't make you 50 times happier.

# One-Planet Living

All this getting and spending is not making our planet happier either. To make our stuff, raw materials are extracted from the Earth. Forests are chopped down by logging and mountains carved up by mining. Tons of electricity and fossil fuels (meaning coal, oil, and gas) are used to run machines and factories.

Raw materials and finished products are then shipped around the world. That shipping uses even more electricity and fossil fuels. Then we burn *more* fossil fuels to get to stores in our cars.

Throughout this entire process, pollution and toxic waste are created and dumped back into the environment—our air, oceans, and forests.

The average American will consume as many resources as 35 average people in India or 53 in China. This is how many Earths we would need if the world's population lived like:

| USA | 5.0 | 🌍 🌍 🌍 🌍 🌍 |
|---|---|---|
| Canada | 4.7 | 🌍 🌍 🌍 🌍 🌑 |
| Australia | 4.1 | 🌍 🌍 🌍 🌑 ◦ |
| UK | 2.9 | 🌍 🌍 🌑 |
| India | 0.7 | 🌑 |
| Global average | 1.7 | 🌍 🌑 |

We are currently using up more resources than the Earth can regenerate each year. That's a planet-sized problem. What's the solution? That's what this book is about.

## EXTREME COLLECTORS

Between 5 and 14 million people in the United States are compulsive hoarders, people who collect and keep so much stuff that it interferes with their daily lives or creates health hazards. Most children enjoy collecting something, like rocks, coins, or stuffed animals. But for some, the urge to collect can become uncontrollable, even in children as young as 11 years old.

People who hoard might get worried and anxious when thinking about what to keep and what to throw away. While some may also suffer from other mental illnesses, many live relatively typical lives. As well, hoarders can learn ways to resist the urge to acquire more stuff.

Some people hoard books, electronic files, or even animals.

# Stuck With Stuff

**AS A KID, I LOVED STUFF.** I collected coins, rocks, cards, stamps, action figures, little cardboard milk caps called "pogs," anything! My family was living below the poverty line, and I was embarrassed about that. I thought my stuff would impress my friends. The paint was peeling off our house and our car was rusty. But hey, I had the most Beanie Babies!

I had about 700 Beanie Babies, including 13 of the exact same monkey, Bongo. But this turtle was much more interesting.

trash the planet with my stuff anymore. I started to get rid of my things.

I went through everything I owned. I asked myself if each thing was bringing value to my life or taking away time and money. I considered whether I'd used it in the last six to twelve months. If not, I got rid of it. I took a lot to thrift stores or gave it away or sold it. What couldn't be donated went to recycling or the landfill (which was my last resort). I did this for a few years and continuously halved my stuff until I got down to 111 possessions.

## Big Stuff, Big Money

As I got older, my stuff got bigger and more expensive. I bought a car—two!—and a boat. To pay for it all, I worked long hours.

After college, I started traveling. For five months, I carried everything I needed in my backpack. And I learned I didn't need as much as I'd thought I did.

Around this time, I was also reading and learning about the impact of my actions on the world around me. I thought, "Hey, I'm spending all my time making money to buy more stuff." It didn't make sense. I wanted to be free. I didn't want to

## Small Space, Less Stuff

I watched *The Story of Stuff* (see link in Resources), which is about how creating, transporting, and disposing of stuff is so destructive. That video really woke me up and motivated me.

Eventually, I got rid of my car. That was a big change. Without a trunk, I couldn't carry so much around.

Then I made my living space smaller. I moved from the largest bedroom in my apartment into a closet. It was a challenge to see if I could fit into a space that small.

Here I am in 2020 with my 44 possessions. Sometimes I have more, sometimes less, depending on where I live or what I'm doing, but I always aim to live with less.

Not everyone can or wants to live with only 111 possessions. We're all unique. But is there one thing you could live without? Or two, or a hundred?

Will you find freedom in owning less, like I did? Only you can answer that question.

## SOMETIMES THE LITTLE THINGS ARE THE HARDEST

One of the hardest things to get rid of was small—my smartphone. It was a great tool, but I knew I had an unhealthy relationship with it. I started leaving my phone at home when I went out. That felt good.

At home, though, my phone and I were still connected at the hip. So I did an experiment: I put it in a drawer for a month. And yes, I could live without a phone! Finally, I canceled my cellphone plan. I felt free!

## —WHAT CAN WE DO ABOUT IT?—
# Keep It Simple

**WHEN ROB WENT TRAVELING AND** lived out of his backpack, he discovered he didn't want to be trapped by his stuff. If you think the minimalist life is for you, how do you simplify?

- **Create a place for everything.** If you have a box for games, a shelf for books, and a bin for craft supplies, they'll be easier to find when you need them.

- **Put on a clothing swap** with friends. Donate any unclaimed clothing to a thrift store.

- **Stay positive.** Even if you can only part with one thing today, that's a start.

When you look at your stuff, ask yourself if it's useful or makes you happy. Have you used it in the last six to twelve months? Are you likely to use it soon?

## One Step at a Time

Decluttering will take time and energy—and no, it won't always be fun. It's best to have a plan. Here are some ideas to get you started:

- **You might love to spend a whole day** clearing your room and power purging. Or maybe you can only handle half an hour at a time. Try it both ways to find out what works best for you.

- **Set goals,** even if they're small ("I'll declutter one shelf in my closet").

- **Focus on clearing out** what you no longer use, what's broken, or what you've outgrown. No one's asking you to part with your favorite things.

Volunteers for the Little Free Library movement build public bookcases. By the end of 2019, there were more than 90,000 Little Free Libraries across 91 countries.

## LIVING WITH LESS

Buying less stuff is just as important as getting rid of your excess. How can you resist the temptation? Start by avoiding the mall. Instead, look for other places to meet with friends. Next, really think about what you have before you buy—and then wait 24 hours before you purchase. You might change your mind.

### ~MINIMALIST TEEN~

If not, you probably won't miss it. Could someone else in your family use it? Could you share it with a friend? Maybe you can rent or borrow sports equipment or tools that you only use once in a while.

Not sure you want to get rid of things that were given to you as gifts? Think of it this way: instead of being neglected in your house, the things you donate have a chance to find a meaningful new home and bring value or happiness to someone else. Your unused musical instrument might change someone's life.

Did you find some craft supplies you'd forgotten about? Were you inspired by what you found? It's amazing how clearing up can spark creativity.

Once your room is just the way you like it, find a way to celebrate. Then each time you get something new, get rid of something you already have. That way, your stuff won't pile up again.

**ISABELLA SYREN'S** family committed to living a zero-waste life when she was nine. They slowly made changes, like buying organic food and not using plastic. And even though they live 10 minutes from downtown San Diego, they grow most of their own food. Isabella helps her parents in their backyard garden. She also keeps her stuff to a minimum, including her clothes. "It has taken a few years," she says, "but my friends have come to like my minimal style."

## You Are Trendy

Congratulations! You're now part of a growing trend toward less. Declutter experts and minimalists are popping up everywhere, proudly showing off the mountains of trash bags they're dumping.

Wait a minute! Where's all that trash going? The answer to that question leads us to...

# 2

# WASTE

## —WHAT'S THE ISSUE?—

## There Is No "Away"

•

**CLANG! CLANG! CLANG!** That's the garbage truck rolling through your neighborhood. Maybe it wakes you up, or maybe you never see it because it comes while you're at school. Either way, every minute of every day, trash is being collected, stored, compacted, managed, and processed.

Dealing with all our garbage is a lot of work. The average person creates 1.63 pounds (0.74 kg) of trash a day. That might not sound like much, but multiply that by 7.5 billion people. We produce 6.1 million tons (5.5 mt) of solid waste *every day*.

## How much waste do people in different countries produce?*

| | |
|---|---|
| USA | 4.9 lb (2.24 kg) |
| Canada | 4.3 lb (1.94 kg) |
| Australia | 3.40 lb (1.54 kg) |
| UK | 2.93 lb (1.33 kg) |
| Global average | 1.63 lb (0.74 kg) |

\* Based on national average

# Introducing—Your Trash!

What exactly are we throwing away? Some good stuff, it turns out.

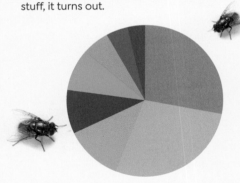

| | |
|---|---|
| 28% | Food and green waste |
| 28% | Paper and cardboard |
| 12% | Plastic |
| 9.3% | Metal |
| 9% | Rubber and leather |
| 5.6% | Wood |
| 4.5% | Glass |
| 3.6% | Other |

If we separated all these materials, our trash would look quite different. We would see a lot of useful resources:

| | | |
|---|---|---|
| **Food and green waste** | → | nutrients for farms and gardens |
| **Paper and cardboard** | → | pulp for new paper products, or material for compost |
| **Metals, wood, and glass** | → | raw materials for new products |

One hundred years ago, most of our household waste was ash (produced from coal burned for heating or cooking) and food scraps, with little or no plastic. Manufactured goods like clothing, toys, furniture, and appliances were well made and expensive to replace, so we fixed them or made do without. Now, we throw them away when they look a little worn or go out of style.

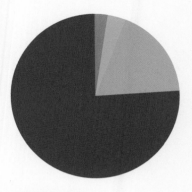

**76%** **Industrial waste**

**18%** **Special waste** (from mining, fuel production, and metals processing)

**3.5%** **Construction and demolition waste**

**2.5%** **Household garbage** (municipal solid waste)

## Garbage Pie

Your household garbage is one tiny slice of the garbage pie. In order to make our stuff—our clothes, food, houses, computers, whatever—farms, mines, mills, and factories generate waste. For every pound (0.45 kg) of trash we put on the curb, between 40 and 70 pounds (18 and 32 kg) were already created just to produce that trash.

Unless you live beside a factory or industrial disposal site, you'll likely never see this industrial waste. What we see is just the tip of the trash iceberg.

## Organized Littering

More than half of our trash is taken to landfills. Landfills have a hugely negative impact on the Earth. They're designed to hold stuff in, not break it down. Even food and grass clippings don't decompose properly. Some landfill excavations have found newspapers that are still readable after 40 years and 20-year-old steaks with meat still on the bones.

The stuff that does break down releases methane, a potent greenhouse gas that contributes to climate change. Other trash is incinerated, which releases some of the most toxic human-made substances known to science into the air.

Landfills are just organized littering. We're turning nature into our trash piles.

But much of our trash doesn't even make it to the landfill. Our oceans, forests, and streets are littered with the stuff. At the rate we're going, by 2050, the plastic in our oceans could weigh more than all the fish.

## Is Recycling the Answer?

Recycling is better than throwing our waste in the landfill, but it's not a good solution. For starters, up to 90 percent of what we throw into recycling bins doesn't actually get recycled. Much of it gets contaminated and is sent to landfills. Some plastics are not recyclable at all, because they're made of mixed materials that are hard to separate.

Recycling does reduce the need to extract new resources, but recycling trucks and plants use a lot of fossil fuels, electricity, and water to collect, clean, and process materials. Even worse, a lot of recycling is shipped to the other side of the world on barges, where it pollutes other countries and forces other people to deal with it.

# Trash Me

**IMAGINE CARRYING AROUND EVERY PIECE** of trash you create. Most of us throw it away without thinking. Out of sight, out of mind. I wanted to know what it would look like to hold on to every piece of trash I created for an entire month. What better way than to wear it?

For many of us, most of our trash comes from the packaged, processed foods we eat.

## Living an Average Life

Once I had my suit, I walked the streets of New York City and lived like everyone else: shopping, eating packaged foods, meeting with friends, and creating garbage just like the average American. Every day, I put the trash suit on before I left the apartment and took it off when I got back.

I wore both recyclables and non-recyclables. Even though 75 percent of what we waste is recyclable under our current system, we as individuals only actually recycle about 30 percent of it. At home the suit sat on a mannequin—until the mannequin broke under the weight after just a week. Then I had to wear it as well!

The artist and environmental advocate Nancy Judd made me a special suit that could hold a month's worth of trash.

## What About the Smell?

I cleaned everything before wearing it. Don't worry, toilet paper went down the toilet. We waste about 20 percent of the food we buy, so I wasted the same amount. I weighed it and replaced it with dry rice.

Eating junk food and carrying all that weight around left me feeling not-so-great. And I wasn't able to do the simple things I love, such as lie on the grass or feel the air on my skin. Wearing the suit was tiring. A few times, I didn't even leave the house. But that wasn't good for my health either.

Day after day the trash became heavier and bulkier. I was truly shocked at how it added up. I couldn't help but imagine how much trash we each create in one year, one decade, or one lifetime.

It was hard for me to last a whole 30 days—so imagine how the planet feels serving as the trash suit for the entire human race.

By the end of the month I realized we all can have a hugely positive impact by making changes in our own lives. In our lifetime we can leave behind a small mountain of trash, or no mountain at all. It starts with one small change. Then another, and another. We each have the power to transform our lives, our communities, and the Earth for the better.

I spoke to fourth and fifth graders in two New York schools. I'm amazed at how so many of them are so conscious of our current situation. When I was a kid, I didn't know about these problems and solutions yet!

# Toward Zero Waste

**DO YOU THINK *YOU* COULD** carry all of your trash, like Rob did? Before you try your own Trash Me experiment, see if you can measure how much you waste in an average week.

Every month, the Future Kids club cleans up their local beach in Cape Town, South Africa. In just over two years, they removed over 4,500 pounds (2,000 kilos) of beach trash.

## The Weight of Your Waste

For a week, put all your trash into a duffel bag. Include recyclables, but not food waste or liquids. Instead, weigh these and either record their weight or put the same weight of dried rice or beans in your container. Carry your duffel bag as often as you can.

At the end of the week, weigh all your trash. Include the weight of the wasted food and liquid. Do you make as much trash as the average person? More?

Next, sort your trash into piles—plastic bottles, packaging, tin cans, and so on. Which piles are the biggest?

## The Rule of the Three Rs

If this experiment makes you want to reduce your trash, here are some tips for moving toward a zero-waste lifestyle.

1. First, **reduce**. Ask yourself, do I really need this or do I just want this?

2. Then, **reuse** everything you can for as long as you can.

3. If reduce and reuse won't work, make **recycling** your last resort.

There are so many ways to apply the three Rs in your life. Here are some of Rob's favorite recommendations:

### On Your Own

- **Ditch disposable bottled water** and carry your own reusable water bottle.

- **Say no to one-time-use disposable items.** Take reusable alternatives instead, such as a cloth towel rather than paper napkins.

- **Think before you buy.** Do you have enough already?

## JUST SAY NO

Another "R" word is "refuse." Say no to freebies, napkins, plastic cutlery, shopping bags, disposable straws, and cups.

### With an Adult

- **Set up a compost bin** for your food scraps and yard waste.

- **Buy unpackaged food** like fruits and vegetables, and get as much as you can in the bulk section of the grocery store.

- **Purchase used stuff** rather than packaged new stuff.

- **If you can afford it, buy higher-quality stuff** that won't turn into trash. And buy less instead of getting lots of cheaply made stuff.

~ABHI THE ECO SUPERHERO~

**ABHISHEK SHASTRI** convinced his school to put recycling bins in the cafeteria when he was in the second grade. He also became the youngest volunteer ambassador for 5 Gyres to take action against plastic pollution. He gives presentations to schools and community groups and has been interviewed about how to go plastic-free and live a more environmentally friendly life.

## HINTS FOR HOLIDAYS

On average, we create 25 percent more waste over the holidays than normal. How can we celebrate birthdays and holidays in a waste-free way? Instead of giving stuff, you can give experiences. You can give "coupons" with offers to do the dishes or fold the laundry (for parents), or to take a friend somewhere, like skating or swimming.

## Trash to Treasure

Communities are coming up with their own solutions to our wasteful ways. There are over 1,500 Repair Cafés worldwide, where people can fix their broken stuff and learn repair skills from experts. And zero-waste grocery stores sell package-free food. Remember when we first met our trash, on page 14? A quarter of that trash is edible. Why are we throwing away food when so many people in the world go hungry? Turn the page to find out.

# FOOD WASTE

## —WHAT'S THE ISSUE?—

## Food Waste Fiasco

•

**THIS MIGHT SOUND WEIRD** (and even gross), but there's a very important message at the bottom of dumpsters. Just ask Rob—he's an experienced dumpster diver.

It all started on a bike trip when Rob rolled around to the back of a local grocery store to see what he could find. And do you know what was in that store's dumpster? A surprising amount of perfectly good food.

If you look for it, you'll find a lot of edible food in dumpsters, landfills, and garbage cans. In wealthy countries such as the United States, Canada, the United Kingdom, and Australia, we waste a ton of food. Billions of dollars' worth.

Sometimes food is lost to bad weather or disease. Labor shortages during harvest time, changing demand, or canceled orders all lead to food waste on the farm. Misshapen or "ugly" produce is often tossed or left to rot, even when it's perfectly fine to eat.

## NATIONAL FOOD WASTE (US$)

These numbers are almost too big to understand. To put them into perspective, the amount of food wasted annually by just these four countries is $30 billion less per year than it would cost to end world hunger, according to a United Nations estimate.

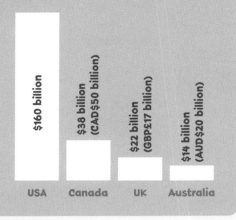

$160 billion — USA

$38 billion (CAD$50 billion) — Canada

$22 billion (GBP£17 billion) — UK

$14 billion (AUD$20 billion) — Australia

## The Food Waste Iceberg

The food in dumpsters is only the tip of the "food waste iceberg." For all the food we waste, even more was lost or wasted before it reached us.

Food spoils when it's stored in conditions that are too warm or too cold, or when there are delays in shipping.

Oversized portions, all-you-can-eat buffets, or strict guidelines about how long food can sit before it's discarded all lead to food waste.

Impulse buying or poor planning can lead to overbuying. Best-by dates (when food can be at its peak freshness or flavor) are often misinterpreted, and people believe the food is bad after these days, when it's not.

Commercial kitchens often prepare too much food, just in case it's needed. Or schools might not allow students to choose parts of a menu or to share untouched foods.

Inefficient processing or mistakes during production can lead to lost food.

## Waste Not, Want Not

What all of this means is that we produce almost twice as much food as we need—all while millions of people go hungry. Around the world, nearly 820 million people don't have enough to eat. This includes one in nine Americans and one in ten Canadians.

We're talking about children too hungry to concentrate at school, elders at home with rumbling tummies, and parents who are working two jobs to make ends meet. It doesn't make sense to waste food while so many people don't have enough.

## Why Worry?

When we waste food, we also waste all of the land, water, fossil fuels, and labor that was used to grow that food. And because we waste so much of it, food waste is one of the leading causes of rainforest deforestation, depletion of fish in the ocean, and biodiversity loss.

# You Need to See It to Believe It

ONE SUMMER, MY FRIEND DANE and I went on a trip. Our adventure wasn't a typical one, though. We decided to cycle across my home state of Wisconsin and only eat food we found in dumpsters.

I've dumpster-dived in at least 100 cities and have almost always found food.

## Supermarket Treasure Chests

Grocery store dumpsters became our treasure chests! You would never guess that the food we were eating came out of the trash. Much of it looked as good as what was inside the store. But I wasn't diving to meet my own needs. Dane and I wanted to show people what we found, so we displayed our treasures in public parks. That got passersby curious and talking. But few people guessed where all that food had been!

I didn't intend to give the food away, but people started taking it home. Box by box, it disappeared. People walked away with smiles, happy with their unexpected bounty of groceries. That made our mission even better.

## New York Dumpsters, Here I Come!

Biking across Wisconsin went so well that I continued cycling all the way to New York City, dumpster diving, displaying food, and photographing along the way. In each city, volunteer drivers helped me, because what I found was too much to carry on my bike. I could roll up in nearly any city across the United States and, in just a day or two, collect enough to feed hundreds of people. My main limitation was often the size of vehicle I had for transport.

The photos I put online helped people across the country to get an idea of the scale of the issue. Many were shocked and even more were angry—not at me, but at the waste our society generates while millions of people go hungry.

Over the course of my tour, we fed about $15,000 worth of food to hundreds of people. All out of dumpsters!

In every single city, nearly every morsel was taken to homes. Young and old, rich and poor, people from all walks of life were eating out of the dumpsters. To me, that's proof that the food is still good.

Even though I biked across seven states eating only wasted food, I still managed to gain weight!

## —WHAT CAN WE DO ABOUT IT?—
# Feed People, Not Landfills

**ROB DOESN'T WANT US ALL** to dumpster dive. He wants us to stop putting food in dumpsters in the first place. At every stage from the farm to our fork, there's a lot we can do to end the Food Waste Fiasco.

Instead of throwing out leftovers or those odds and ends in the fridge, you can add them to soups or stews.

## At Home

Before you go telling anybody else not to waste food, look at your own actions. Does your garbage can have any food in it? Lead by example.

Less is best. Make a habit of helping yourself to less, especially if you're not sure if you like a food, or can't decide if you're hungry or not. You can always get seconds if you're still hungry.

Cut it out. Brown spots or bruises can be cut out of fruit or vegetables. Most times, the rest is still edible.

Compost wasted food. This is a last resort and should be done with food that can no longer be eaten. If you live in an apartment, it's still possible to compost.

### MAKE the BIG CHANGE

### GROW YOUR OWN

When you grow food yourself, you'll feel a deeper connection to it—and you'll probably be excited to eat it, not waste it. You don't need a lot of room. Herbs such as cilantro, basil, and chives can grow in small pots on a balcony or windowsill.

## In the Store

Ask for ugly. We need to put pressure on grocery stores to change. But we can't put all the blame on them. After all, they're trying to meet the demands of their shoppers. We must ask stores to relax their cosmetic standards and stock ugly produce. You can do this by posting messages to with the hashtag #DemandUgly on social media. Once stores change what they stock, farmers won't have to waste their weird-looking, but still tasty, produce.

Ask grocery stores to #DonateNotDump. You can tweet or message them, email them, or go in and talk to the manager. But be informed; see the Resources on page 80.

Support your local farmers. If there's a farmers' market nearby, check it out. Typically, small local farmers waste a lot less food because they appreciate it for what it is—a life-giving substance.

## School Waste

Kids eat at least five meals a week at school. What happens to what they don't eat? In the United States alone, students throw away 1 billion unopened and unpeeled food items each year.

Groups such as K–12 Food Rescue educate US schools on food waste and help them to start food rescue programs, such as sharing tables in school cafeterias, or regular deliveries to local food banks.

With programs like K–12 Food Rescue, unopened packages of food or unpeeled fruit are donated from school cafeterias, like this one, to food pantries. This gives students a better alternative to throwing food into the trash.

— TEEN LEADER —

When GABRIELLE POSARD was 12, she was shocked at how much food is wasted in the United States every year and at how many people don't get enough to eat. At 13, she founded the nonprofit Donate Don't Dump, a teen-led organization that donates surplus food and advocates for grocery stores and other businesses to reduce the amount of food they waste. Since then, the organization has grown to include over 4,000 members. Together, they have rescued over 850,000 pounds (386,000 kg) of food and 650,000 meals.

A hundred years ago, most of us grew some of our own food. We knew where our food came from, and because it took so much work to grow, we valued it and didn't waste it. Now, industrial farms can grow huge amounts of food so we don't have to, but is that always a good thing? Let's find out...

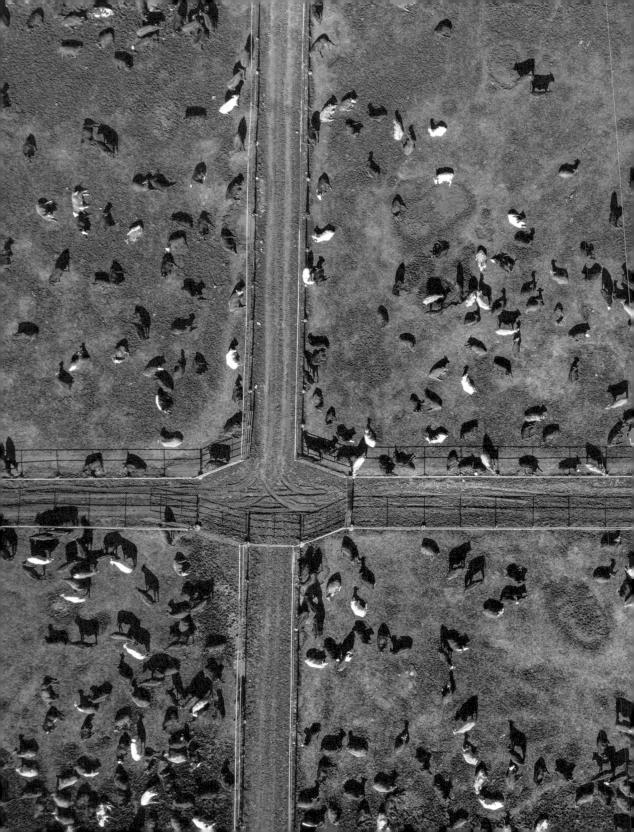

## 4

# THE FOOD SYSTEM

*—WHAT'S THE ISSUE?—*

## The True Cost of Food

•

**WHEN YOU'RE ENJOYING YOUR DINNER,** your food can look pretty innocent. But bite by bite, the food we consume is consuming our planet. We need to wake up to the reality of our broken food system—how our food is grown, harvested, processed, packaged, transported, marketed, eaten, and disposed of.

## Not All Farms Are Created Equal

All food comes from a farm. Even soda pop contains corn, sugar cane, or beet syrup. It takes a lot of land to feed humans the highly processed, high-meat diet many of us have grown used to. Natural lands, like rainforests or prairies, are cleared for farming and grazing animals. Almost half of the land on Earth is farmland or ranchland.

Commercial farms need to produce as much food as possible so that they can make a profit. To do so, they rely on fossil fuels, synthetic fertilizers, and pesticides to grow more, and grow faster. These toxic chemicals then pollute our air, soil, and water, which is harmful to our health when we simply breathe or drink water. Many farmworkers are exposed to higher concentrations of these chemicals every day, and this takes a serious toll on their health.

In our modern factory-based food system, the goal is to raise animals quickly and cheaply. Farm animals fed growth hormones can be ready to sell faster. Vaccines and antibiotics allow farmers to pack more animals into smaller spaces with less risk of diseases caused by crowding (but this creates worse diseases).

## Black Gold

Most farmers need healthy "dirt"—topsoil—for their crops. Healthy topsoil is more than just dirt. It's made up of minerals, organic matter, water, and countless tiny organisms. But we're losing this precious soil largely due to intensive, chemical-heavy farming techniques and the cutting down of forests. Wind or water carry topsoil. Unsustainable farming techniques, such as the overuse of chemicals, or allowing farm animals to overgraze, result in unhealthy topsoil.

## Addicted to Convenience

Raw, whole foods are shipped to factories, which are often far away from the farms. There, they are milled, pressed, cooked, canned, filtered, extracted, irradiated, fermented, dried, rehydrated, baked, homogenized, or bleached.

All of this processing consumes energy, and creates waste when the unwanted food is discarded. And heavily processed foods are not as healthy for us as whole foods.

Raw ingredients are mixed with stabilizers and other chemicals to improve their taste or stop them from spoiling. Most of us have no idea how toxic all the unfamiliar ingredients in processed food might be.

Our ultra-processed diet is a leading cause of obesity, diabetes, and high blood pressure. These health problems are either rare or unknown in societies that eat simple, unprocessed foods.

## A Not-So-Tidy Package

Processed foods are sealed in packaging and shipped to stores. Most of that packaging ends up in landfills, but a shocking amount ends up in lakes and rivers and eventually oceans. During one annual international beach cleanup, nine out of ten pieces of garbage found were related to food or drink. As a result, marine animals get trapped or injured in plastic loops or other objects. Or they mistake the plastic for food and eat it. When large creatures eat smaller ones, this plastic works its way up the food chain and into fish or seafood that we might eat.

Plastic lingers in our landfills, oceans, and waterways for a long time. Heat and light breaks plastic down into smaller pieces, but when it's buried in landfills or sinks down to the ocean floor, it breaks down much more slowly.

Think about eating a bag of potato chips. You might take five minutes to eat the chips, but how long will it take for that bag to disintegrate completely? We don't know, because plastic hasn't been around long enough. It could take hundreds or even thousands of years.

### FOOD AND ENERGY

It takes a lot of energy to grow plants and raise animals for food under this system. Farm vehicles such as tractors burn gas or diesel. Other equipment, like water pumps, use electricity. Energy is used to grow animal feed such as corn or soy. Mining and manufacturing fertilizers require energy. Finally, processing, packaging, shipping, and disposing of food uses up even more energy.

When fossil fuels such as gas or oil are burned to make this energy, they release greenhouse gases like carbon dioxide, methane, and nitrous oxide. These gases rise up and make our atmosphere warmer. In total, animals raised for food are one of the leading sources of the world's greenhouse gases.

Our current food system basically turns fossil fuels into food. But there are alternatives—alternatives that are healthy for the planet, our communities, and other species.

# —WHAT DID ROB DO?—
# Food Freedom

**THROUGH MY DUMPSTER DIVING EXPERIENCES,** I learned that I could live completely off food wasted by our global, industrial food system. But I was still curious. I wanted to know if I could live without relying on that system at all.

Could I grow and forage 100 percent of my food? And could I completely avoid packaging, processed food, food that was shipped long distances, and food that was sprayed with chemicals? Could I do all this for a full year?

## Total Immersion

I've found no better way to understand an issue than to fully immerse myself in it. Our globalized food system is so complex, with so many steps between the farms and our plates, that it's difficult to feel a genuine connection to the food we eat.

So I spent a year growing, foraging, and making all my food. That's more than 1,000 meals in a row!

## What Does 100 Percent Really Mean?

When I say 100 percent, I really mean it! No grocery stores, no restaurants, not even a cookie from a friend's pantry or a soda at a party. I had to grow all of my meals, including every snack and dessert, and even had to harvest my medicine.

## Steep Learning Curve

I hadn't grown much food before, so the first step was to figure out what grew well in Florida, where I was living at the time, and what I could harvest locally. I didn't own any land, so I worked with volunteers to turn their lawns into gardens and we shared the harvest.

Before…

After!

## What Did I Eat?

Over the year, I grew more than 100 foods and foraged nearly 200. And after 365 days, I maintained my weight and came out healthier than when I started.

I grew a lot of sweet potatoes—500 pounds (227 kg) of them! And even then, I ran out. I often ate a couple of pounds (1 kg) of greens a day or made green juice. Greens were my nutritional powerhouse. Fruit was my go-to snack. I ate more than 50 different kinds of fruits, so I never got bored. For protein, I ate beans and peas, deer, and fish that I caught from the ocean, lakes, and rivers. Many vegetables have protein in them too.

I foraged for coconuts, which are good for fat and calories, and made my own coconut milk, oil, and coconut butter. I was nervous about how I'd get salt, which our bodies need to function properly. But it was as simple as scooping up ocean water and boiling it on my stove until the water evaporated, leaving salt behind. I kept honeybees and harvested honey from their hives. I've got a sweet tooth, so I knew I'd need honey.

This project was about inspiring and empowering others to grow some food. With friends, I provided gardens for 15 people in my community, planted more than 200 Community Fruit Trees, and sent out 5,000 Free Seed Packs. People everywhere were growing food!

# —WHAT CAN WE DO ABOUT IT?—
# The Planet-Friendly Diet

**MOST OF US CAN'T GROW AND FORAGE** all our food like Rob did. But he does encourage us to discover where our food comes from. If we don't like what we find, then we can change.

There are many ways to eat healthy food, reduce your impact on the planet, save money, and align your food choices with your ethics. Some of the suggestions below might require help from an adult, but some you can do on your own.

## On Your Own

- **Eat more plants** such as vegetables, fruits, grains, nuts, and seeds.

- **Remember to not waste food** and to compost whatever can't be eaten.

- **Make it yourself.** If your parents don't have the time to cook from scratch, could you help them out? Find a simple recipe for smoothies or bread or granola bars instead of relying on store-bought versions. Your home cooking will be cheaper, tastier, and healthier (because you can put in whole foods and leave out additives and preservatives). Cooking from scratch also lets you tailor the recipe to your own taste. Make a big batch and freeze the extra in reusable containers. Or share it with a neighbor.

**MAKE the BIG CHANGE**

## WHAT CAN YOU FORAGE?

Foods are growing freely and abundantly all around us. Even many weeds are edible. In some areas, community harvest programs make use of fruit or vegetables that would otherwise go to waste. In others, fruit trees are planted by local groups. Explore whether these options are available in your neighborhood, or take a foraging class to learn what is edible in your area.

You can forage for wild garlic leaves and flowers. They'll make a salad extra tasty.

## With an Adult

- **Shop locally** and buy food that was grown locally. Talk to your family about affordable ways to eat local food. Is there a farmers' market or food co-op nearby? If not, your family can still buy fewer imported foods. This might mean trying foods you've never eaten before. Look for those little stickers on your produce—where was it grown?

- **Pick whole foods** instead of processed. These are foods with one ingredient, not a long list.

- **Buy natural, organic foods** when possible. Avoid GMOs—foods that have been genetically modified. If you eat meat, eggs, and dairy, look for options that weren't produced on factory farms.

- **Grow some of your own food.** If you don't have the space for a garden, find out if there's a community garden nearby that you can join.

## ~SEED LIBRARIAN~

As soon as **ALICIA SERRATOS** learned about seed libraries, she loved the idea. Instead of checking out books, seed libraries check out seeds. Borrowers can sample seeds for free. Harvested seeds are then returned to the library. To earn her Girl Scout Silver Award, Alicia created the 3 Sisters Seed Box, which includes everything needed to start your own seed library. Her goal was to distribute 100 boxes across the United States.

With a shift in perspective, all of these positive steps can come naturally. And by eating in a way that's better for the planet, we'll find ourselves happier and healthier too! Our current food system is broken largely because our food has been turned into a for-profit industry. Rob believes food is a life-giving substance and a human right, just like water. Read on to find out more about that...

# WATER

## —WHAT'S THE ISSUE?—

## Wasting Water

**•**

**FOR FIVE HOT SUMMER DAYS,** Rob lived solely off water from a leaky fire hydrant in New York City. He drank from it, bathed in it, did his laundry in it, and brushed his teeth in it. One day, he timed how long it took to fill a one-gallon (3.8 L) jug. It took two minutes, which meant that over 700 gallons (2,650 L) of water was being wasted from that hydrant alone, every day the leak continued. A person only needs to drink about half a gallon (1.9 L) of water a day to survive. So that NYC hydrant leaked enough water to meet the drinking needs of over 1,440 people every day.

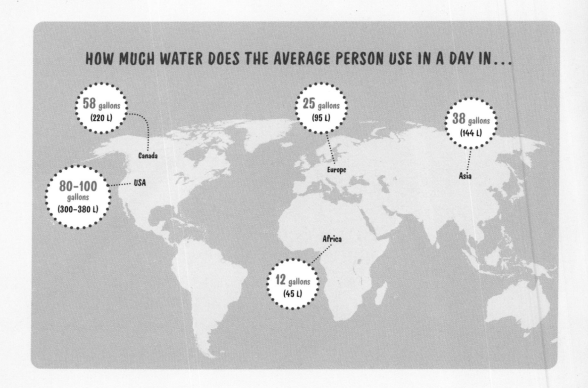

# 5

## HOW MUCH WATER DOES THE AVERAGE PERSON USE IN A DAY IN...

**58** gallons (220 L)

Canada

**80–100** gallons (300–380 L)

USA

**25** gallons (95 L)

Europe

**38** gallons (144 L)

Asia

Africa

**12** gallons (45 L)

## How Much Water Do We Use?

The leaky hydrant was an obvious example of water waste, but the truth is, we waste water every day, especially compared to many other parts of the world.

The graphic above shows just what we use in our homes, such as when we flush the toilet, wash our clothes, shower, or run the faucet. During hot weather we can use a lot more water outside our homes than inside, by watering a lawn, washing a car, or filling a backyard pool. The water we use outdoors can reach up to 80 percent of our home water use.

## But Wait! There's More!

We use water in hundreds of other ways too. In fact, our home water use accounts for only *5 percent* of our total water use. Driving a car or surfing the web uses water. The items we buy at the store also use water. How? As we've learned, water is needed to grow, make, and transport our things and food. It's also used to create energy.

**How much water is used to make...?***

**1 FACTORY-FARMED BURGER**

**635 gallons**
(2,400 L)

**1 TOMATO**

**13 gallons**
(50 L)

**1 COTTON T-SHIRT**

**660 gallons**
(2,500 L)

**1 CHOCOLATE BAR**

**450 gallons**
(1,700 L)

**1 EGG**

**50 gallons**
(190 L)

**GAS** GASOLINE

**70 gallons**
(265 L)

* These numbers are "water footprints." They measure how much fresh water is used to grow, make, and deliver something to you.

Dirt or oil from sidewalks, roads, and highways can wash into rivers and lakes.

And while the same amount of water exists on Earth today as when the Earth first formed, much of our fresh water is becoming not so fresh. Factories, farms, and cities all create pollution—from big pieces of trash to unseen toxins—which can wash into our lakes, rivers, and oceans or seep into our groundwater. Water is essential to all life, which means water pollution harms us all: people, animals, and plants.

The good news is that there are some simple solutions we all can adopt, starting today.

## Why Does It Matter?

You might think, "Water just gets recycled; it doesn't get wasted. Why does it matter?"

When we waste water, we also waste the resources that went into that water—the electricity and fossil fuels needed to pump it to us, and the chemicals used to treat the water both before and after it flows through our faucets.

We need clean water in order to live. Do you think having access to clean water is a basic human right?

## —WHAT DID ROB DO?—
# Water Wise Living

**ON MY FIRST BIKE RIDE** across the United States, one of my goals was to use as little water as possible. What I did use came from natural sources such as rivers, lakes, rain, or wells. Or I used water that was going to waste, from sources like leaky faucets or broken sprinklers. I purified what I drank with a portable water filter so it was safe. Over the 104 days of that ride, I used about 160 gallons (600 L) of water, which works out to about 1.5 gallons (roughly 6 L) a day—far less than what the average American uses each day.

I bathed in natural sources of water, or in wasted water (like from the leaky fire hydrant). I didn't shower once.

Even though it was a hot summer, I felt great—and clean. I decided I wouldn't shower for another six months. Six months turned into one year. One year turned into two years. How long could I go without a shower?

Water that has been used—for example, in the bath or to wash dishes—is often called "greywater." If it isn't too dirty, it can be reused for watering plants or for things like flushing the toilet.

## Harvesting Water in the Teeny Greeny

Some time after my bike trip, I moved into a 50-square-foot (4.65 m²) house, the Teeny Greeny, in San Diego, California. The state was in the middle of a 10-year megadrought. I decided I wanted to use as little water as possible to set an example.

Even though I lived in the city, my house was off the grid. That meant I had no water or electricity from the municipality. Instead of turning on a tap, I harvested rainwater. Rain ran from the roof into a gutter and then into storage barrels. I only needed one five-gallon (19 L) jug a day.

I filtered all my drinking water, like I did on my bike trip. Rainwater is one of my favorite drinks!

## Love Every Drop

Whenever possible, I used water more than once. When I washed dishes, the greywater drained into a bucket under the sink. My dishwater then watered my veggie garden.

And I still didn't shower. I swam in the ocean or, on cold days, heated water on the stove and then scrubbed down with a hot towel.

I didn't waste a single drop at home.

## My First Shower in 1,000 Days

I knew I had to end my no-shower stretch at some point. Five years sounded good, but I didn't feel like waiting that long. But 1,000 seemed like a good, round number.

For over two years, I'd been blogging about not showering. On the 1,000th day, my first shower was captured on video and broadcast live on social media before my TEDxTeen Talk in London.

I didn't want to waste 1.6 gallons (6.1 L) of water every time I flushed, so I used a composting toilet. It uses no water at all. Just a handful of sawdust, so no smell! The waste turned into humanure, which could be used for compost on fruit trees.

# —WHAT CAN WE DO ABOUT IT?—
# Be Water Wise

**DOES ROB WANT US ALL** to stop showering? No, he wants us to appreciate our water and use it wisely. Here are some ways we can do that.

You can reuse rinse water by placing a bowl in the sink. This water can be used to flush the toilet or for plants.

- **Fewer, shorter showers.** Every minute you shave off your shower will save about two gallons (7.5 L) of water. Shut off the water while you scrub down, and then turn it on to rinse off.

- **Turn off the faucet.** When you brush your teeth, turn off the faucet after you wet your toothbrush. This can save up to five gallons (19 L) of water every time.

Many people around the world don't have water in their homes, so they have to collect it every day from an outside source. Try carrying two large jugs (1 gallon/3.8 L each). How long can you last?

## On Your Own

- **Eat more veggies, fewer industrial animals.** You can save up to 600 gallons (2,271 L) of water a day by eating more plant-based foods instead of factory-farmed animals.

- **Wash clothes less often.** Wait until you have a full load before you run the washing machine. A bonus? Your clothes will last longer if you wash them less frequently.

- **Flush less often.** If it's yellow let it mellow. If it's brown flush it down. You can also put a bottle of sand or a brick in the toilet tank to displace water. With each flush, you'll save that volume of water.

## With an Adult

- **Grow food, not lawns.** If you turn your lawn into a garden, you'll cut back on your water usage drastically. And you can grow your own food!

- **Install water-efficient faucets,** showerheads, appliances, and toilets. This helps to cut back on water usage without having to change your habits.

- **Fix leaks.** Drips waste far more water than you might imagine. A leaky toilet can waste 200 gallons (757 L) of water per day.

- **Sweep or scrub.** Try to not use water to wash your car, driveway, sidewalk, or house. A dry towel or a broom will often get the job done. Avoid using power washers.

- **Plant natives.** Grow plants that are adapted to the climate of your area. Turn your grassy lawn into a native prairie or a beautiful patch of wild-flowers for the bees.

## ~SPEAKING UP FOR WATER~

**AUTUMN PELTIER** believes that water should have the same rights and protections as human beings. She has been advocating for water since she was eight years old. At 13, she challenged a room of United Nations diplomats to protect water for future generations. A year later, she became the Chief Water Commissioner for the Anishinabek First Nation and continues to work hard to protect the Great Lakes.

### MAKE the BIG CHANGE

### MAKE THE MOST OF EVERY DROP

Find ways to repurpose your water. Try rinsing your produce in a bowl, then use the water on your garden. Or keep a big bowl in your tub and reuse your shower or bathwater to flush the toilet. Can you think of other ways?

These tips don't cover all the ways we use water, but by trying them out, you can easily cut your usage in half or more.

To cut your energy use even further, start powering down. Are you wondering how that works? Read on to find out.

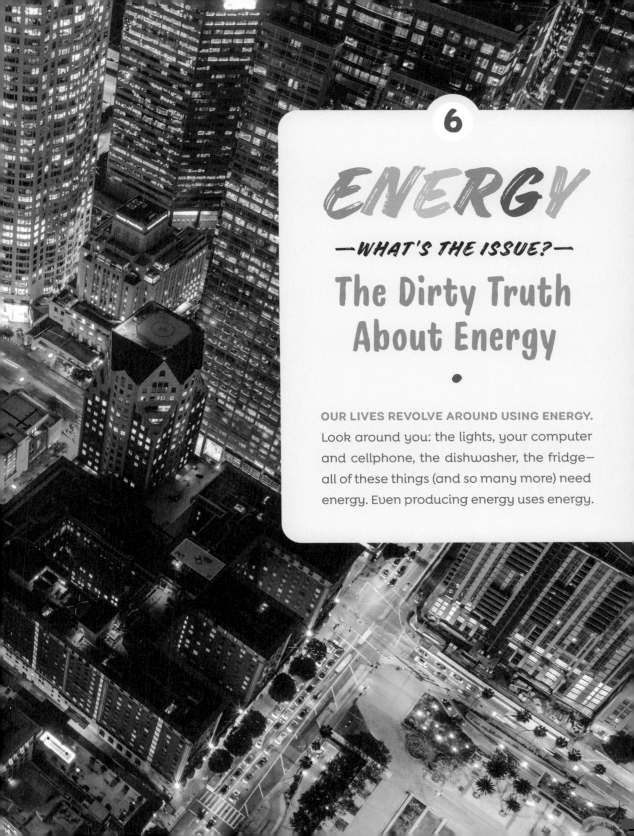

# 6

## ENERGY

### —WHAT'S THE ISSUE?—

## The Dirty Truth About Energy

•

**OUR LIVES REVOLVE AROUND USING ENERGY.**
Look around you: the lights, your computer
and cellphone, the dishwasher, the fridge—
all of these things (and so many more) need
energy. Even producing energy uses energy.

## Where Does Energy Come From?

We get energy from many different sources. Most cars use gas, which is a fossil fuel. Lights, heaters, refrigerators, and computers use electricity.

Electricity is what's known as secondary energy source because it has to be generated from a primary energy source, such as the sun, wind, fossil fuels, moving water, or nuclear power. Where does the energy you use come from?

## TWO KINDS OF ENERGY

Energy sources are either renewable or nonrenewable. Fossil fuels (oil, gas, and coal) are made from plants and animals that lived millions of years ago. It takes millions of years to make new fossil fuels. Nuclear energy is made from a rare type of uranium. We call these energies "nonrenewable."

Sun, wind, and water can't be used up, because they're naturally replenished. (Though polluted water is, of course, less useful than pure, clean water.) They're called "renewable energies."

## Clean Energy, Dirty Energy

All forms of energy have an impact on our planet, but some are more harmful than others, depending on how the energy is created and whether using it leads to pollution or not. When it comes to being kind to the planet, no energy source is perfect. But some are kinder than others.

## WHAT ARE GREENHOUSE GASES?

When fossil fuels burn, they release greenhouse gases (GHGs) into the air, which trap heat in our atmosphere. This contributes to changes in climate around the world and extreme weather (such as floods, droughts, forest fires, or storms). To avoid the worst effects of these changes, we would benefit from using fossil fuels a lot less and renewable energies a lot more.

- **Mining for coal** can pollute rivers and fill them with mining debris. To get to the coal, open pits are carved into the land, or the top of mountains are chopped off. The waste rock and dirt are then dumped. Transporting coal is expensive and requires energy. Burning coal produces GHGs (mostly carbon dioxide) and toxic ash.

- **Oil pumps** are often powered by gas. Sometimes water is injected into the ground to force the oil up, which pollutes the water. Refining the crude oil and transporting it is expensive and requires a lot of energy. Millions of gallons of oil are spilled every year, on land or in the ocean, harming animals and ecosystems. Finally, burning oil releases GHGs into our air.

- **Hydraulic fracturing** (or "fracking") makes it possible to reach previously inaccessible stores of oil and gas. But fracking frequently contaminates groundwater, pollutes land with chemicals, leaks methane into the air, and even causes earthquakes.

- **Nuclear energy** generates electricity by breaking up atoms of uranium. The mining, refining, and transportation of uranium requires energy and also releases GHGs. As well, nuclear power creates radioactive waste, which lasts millions or billions of years and is often stored unsafely.

- **Hydroelectricity** is renewable, because water is not destroyed when it runs through the turbines. It also creates fewer emissions than burning fossil fuels. But building dams changes rivers and floods valleys, which can force communities to relocate, degrades water quality, and harms the plants and animals that live in the river as well as the surrounding environment.

- **Renewable energy** sources like wind, geothermal, and solar produce electricity with less pollution and lower carbon emissions than fossil fuels. However, we still need to mine for the materials to make the windmills, solar panels, and storage batteries. Maybe future societies will look back and think these were "dirty" energy sources.

- Some **biofuels** make use of organic material that would otherwise go to waste, but others, called first-generation biofuels, are made from crops (such as palm oil, corn, or soy) grown specifically for fuel. Forests are being cleared to grow first-generation biofuels, which means they aren't planet-friendly after all.

Sadly, we use a lot more of the harmful energies (like fossil fuels) than the kinder ones (renewables). As we become more aware of the drawbacks of fossil fuels, and as the costs of renewable energies fall, we are changing quickly. We're in the middle of an energy revolution.

We can't stop using energy altogether. But we can use less of it (much less!), and we can use cleaner and more renewable energy instead of dirtier energy.

# —WHAT DID ROB DO?—
# Unplug

**I'VE GONE TO SOME PRETTY EXTREME MEASURES** to discover how electricity is woven into my life. For one summer, I stripped my life back to the absolute basics and observed my actions. This helped me to understand how I was using energy every second of the day and night.

I bicycled across the United States off the grid, using only electricity I generated myself. That meant not turning on a single light, using a fan or air-conditioning, cooking in a kitchen, or using any other device that was not powered by electricity I created. If I wanted to walk into a store that only had automatic doors, I had to wait until someone else was walking in and then walk in with them. I had two small solar panels to charge my electronics: my laptop, cellphone, bike lights, and headlamp.

I only plugged into five outlets all summer, when I ran out of solar energy but still wanted to share the story of my journey through social media.

I have also cooked with a propane stove. Because propane tanks have a finite supply, I use as little as possible.

One energy-free way to store fresh food is to ferment it. My homemade sauerkraut adds delicious flavor to meals.

## Living Small

Next, I lived in a tiny house in San Diego, California, off the grid. I had drastically reduced my need for electricity, so the little bit I did need—for my laptop and lights—came from two small solar panels. I cooked over a rocket stove built out of salvaged bricks, with wood from fallen branches for fuel. I cut out the need for a fridge by buying only a few days' worth of produce at a time and using dry goods.

## Our Electrified Lives

In each of these situations, I had to find a simple, sustainable way to create energy. We all live in different situations and have different needs, so our solutions will differ. But the first step is to become aware of how much energy we use, and think of ways to use less.

By limiting how much energy I have access to, I've learned how truly electrified my life was. So much of what we do uses electricity. For many of us, that means burning fossil fuels to make that electricity.

When electricity is available at the flip of a switch, we needlessly consume it. It's too easy to waste a lot without ever thinking twice.

Most of us aren't going to unplug completely, but we can all cut back on our usage without reducing our quality of life. In doing so, we can reduce our environmental impact hugely, while also saving a lot of money.

# Lighten Up

**THERE ARE MANY WAYS TO** become energy sippers instead of energy guzzlers. To start, grab a notebook and, for one day, write down every time you use electricity or any other kind of energy.

Here are more ways to lighten up:

- **Find out where your electricity comes from.** Is it from coal, nuclear, water, or natural gas?

- **Research which cleaner energies are available** in your area, or if your community has a renewable energy co-op that you could join.

- **Challenge yourself** to use electricity only five or ten times in one day. Can you do it?

- **Choose one or two things you can do** this week to use less energy. Read on for some ideas.

- **Once you master one new habit,** move on to the next. It might take months or years to unplug your life, but that's okay. Bettering yourself is about constantly making small improvements.

## Less Is Best

You can find lots of tips for using less electricity once you start looking. Here are a few of Rob's suggestions for less obvious ways.

- **Use less water.** It takes energy to clean our water, heat it, and, most of the time, to pump it to us. According to the Environmental Protection Agency, a faucet running for five minutes uses enough energy to power a 60-watt light bulb for 18 hours. Check chapter 5 for suggestions on how to use less water.

**MAKE** *the* **BIG CHANGE**

### USE YOUR HUMAN POWER

***You*** are a source of energy. Bike, walk, wheel, or skateboard instead of sitting in a car. Play board games instead of video or online games. Sweep the floor with a broom instead of using the vacuum. What other people-powered solutions can you think of?

- **Improve your diet.** Growing, processing, and transporting our food uses a lot of energy. Be more planet-friendly by eating more locally produced and whole foods. You'll find other ideas for energy-efficient eating in chapter 4.

- **Waste less.** Energy was used to make everything we throw away: food, clothing, games, paper, electronics. So let's stop throwing it away! We also waste energy when we leave gadgets and appliances running. Turn off everything that doesn't need to be on, like taps, lights, or the computer. Even better, unplug electronics when you're not using them.

- **Get outside.** When we spend less time on our gadgets, the more time we have to go outside into the beautiful world, which is powered by the sun.

## ~POO POWER~

**SEVERAL ZOOS** in Europe and North America are turning zoo poo into power. Holding tanks, called biodigesters, convert animal waste into biogas, which can be used like natural gas or turned into power in a generator. The Toronto Zoo biogas project, which is a nonprofit co-op, also adds food waste to the mix. Big animals = big poo = big power.

## THE PRICE OF POWER

Many of us think that greener energies are too expensive, but in 2015 the world's fossil-fuel industry received $10 million a minute in grants or subsidies (money granted by governments to help the industry). And then there are hidden costs to fossil fuels, like health costs from exposure to air pollution, environmental damage, traffic congestion, or the destruction caused by extreme weather events. Subsidies make it seem like fossil fuels are cheaper, but we're all paying the true price.

The added benefit of using your own energy is that you get exercise too. Check out the next chapter to find out how getting from A to B affects the planet.

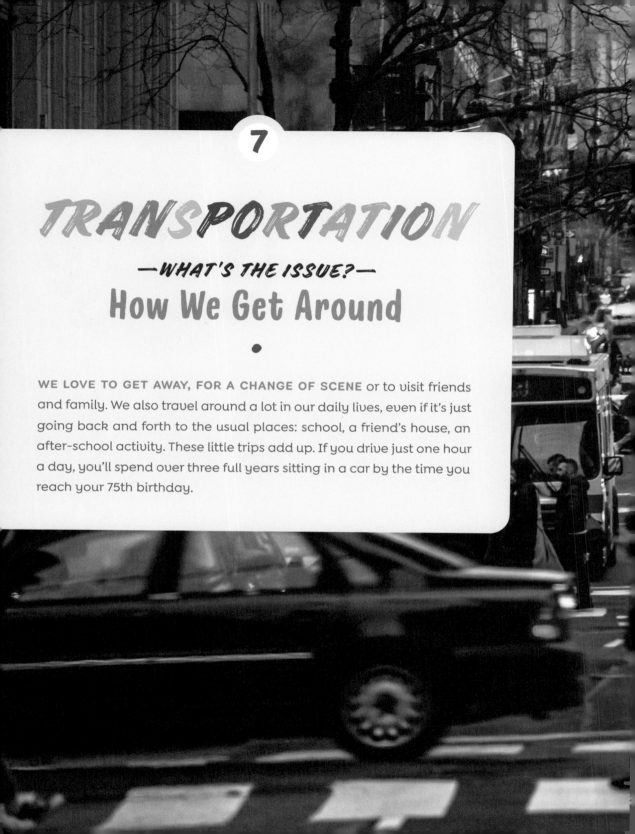

# 7

# TRANSPORTATION

## —WHAT'S THE ISSUE?—

## How We Get Around

•

**WE LOVE TO GET AWAY, FOR A CHANGE OF SCENE** or to visit friends and family. We also travel around a lot in our daily lives, even if it's just going back and forth to the usual places: school, a friend's house, an after-school activity. These little trips add up. If you drive just one hour a day, you'll spend over three full years sitting in a car by the time you reach your 75th birthday.

## Measuring Our Moves

How we get around—for short trips or long ones—has a huge impact on the Earth, our community, and ourselves. Transportation, which includes commercial shipping as well as our individual travel, creates about one-fifth of the world's greenhouse gas (GHG) emissions. That figure is even higher in most industrialized countries like the United States and Canada, where it's almost 30 percent of our GHG emissions.

## Jetting Around

We don't travel by plane as often as we do by car, but air travel has one of the highest impacts on the environment. Jets need a lot of fuel to fly and their emissions are particularly damaging because they are released high in the atmosphere.

## Car Culture

Cars are convenient, but convenience comes at a cost. Most of a car's carbon and water footprint comes from the gas it uses. When gas is burned, the carbon dioxide and tiny carbon particles in the exhaust pollute our air. Because tailpipes are at street level, the polluted air from the fuel cars burn goes directly into our lungs.

Cars can also be expensive. New cars cost anywhere from $6,000 to $10,000 a year to own, and still their value goes down every year. Most of that money is spent on gas, but payments, insurance, and maintenance (and don't forget parking tickets!) are all additional costs.

Cars affect the way we design our communities too. Six-lane freeways are great for getting cars around, but terrible for people who want to walk or bike. Freeways aren't even good for the people in the cars. Drivers often get angry or frustrated in traffic. Exposure to pollution from traffic causes respiratory problems like asthma, especially in children. And all that sitting, instead of using our bodies to move, isn't good for our health.

On top of this, it's harder to meet our neighbors and other people in our community when we're stuck inside a car. Walking, biking, and taking public transit give us more opportunities to start conversations, connect with people, and feel part of the community (see chapter 9 on connection).

A turtle naturally defends itself by drawing into its shell, but when the threat is an oncoming car, this behavior makes them especially vulnerable to being crushed.

For many wildlife populations, cars and roads are one of the biggest causes of death.

## The Road Beneath Our Tires

Roads also have a big impact on our environment, and not just when wilderness is cleared to build them. In the United States alone, over a million animals die on roads every day. As well, roadways break up an animal's habitat. They also prevent them from traveling freely, which makes finding a mate, water, or food harder. Pollution from exhaust, oil, tire debris, and de-icing salts can also harm animals, and noise and lights from cars can confuse or disorient them.

## WHAT'S THE BEST WAY TO GET AROUND?

The numbers below show how much energy is used for one person to travel one mile or kilometer.*

| | |
|---|---|
| Cycling | 0.03 / 0.06 |
| Walking | 0.07 / 0.16 |
| City bus | 0.41 / 0.92 |
| Motorcycle | 0.77 / 1.73 |
| Gas car | 0.94 / 2.10 |
| Long-haul aircraft | 1.08 / 2.42 |

\* Average kilowatt-hours per passenger mile/ megajoules per passenger kilometer.

# Life on a Bike

**I GOT MY FIRST CAR** when I was 16. I thought it was my ticket to freedom. With a car, I could go where I wanted, when I wanted. And it was a huge part of my social status. I couldn't imagine my life without it.

Then I started learning more about what was going on with our world. I started to feel uncomfortable pumping fuel into my car. Not only was I spending a lot of money on gas, but the gas I bought contributed to war, oil spills, and pollution.

## Sold My Car, Bought My Freedom

I thought hard about the advantages and disadvantages of selling my car. Without it, I would save money, exercise more, and shop less often in big-box stores. I'd also be living according to my beliefs. But I wouldn't be able to go wherever I wanted, whenever. I'd have to bike in bad weather, and it would be harder to transport lots of stuff.

In the end, there seemed to be more advantages to living without a car, so I sold it. I bought a really nice bike and a membership in an electric car-share program.

I've never looked back. I enjoy all the advantages I'd anticipated, and I adapted to the disadvantages more easily than I thought I would. And it was so much easier to make other environmental changes without a car. Plus, I was in the best shape of my life.

I even got the crazy idea to bike across the United States.

## Off the Grid Across the United States

I bought a bamboo bike and a trailer with solar panels for the trip. This ride wasn't just for fun (though it was), but to raise awareness about sustainability and create positive change.

The 4,700-mile (7,564 km) trip, from San Francisco to Waitsfield, Vermont, took 104 days. Over the entire journey, I plugged into only five outlets and never turned on a light switch. I created two pounds (0.9 kg) of trash, nine pounds (4.1 kg) of recycling, and composted all of my food scraps. I took just one ferry ride into Manhattan, and didn't use any other fossil fuels for transportation.

At times, the trip was grueling. On the first day, I realized the trailer was too heavy, so I had to get rid of a lot of stuff. Nevada was much colder, mountainous, and lonelier than I'd expected, and I was freezing! Headwinds made crossing Kansas especially tough. And from New York to Boston,

I had to ride during a heat wave. I learned that when you have less, but appreciate it, it feels like more. I appreciated a small sip of water, a morsel of food, the last 3 percent of battery life on my laptop, clean clothes, fresh air, smooth roads, and fresh water to swim in.

I learned so much and met so many people I wouldn't have met otherwise. Life is good when you're on a bike.

### OIL WARS

Ever since World War I, we've been fighting over oil. Countries with large reserves of oil have power, because other countries want that oil and the energy it produces. Oil-rich countries with unstable governments are also 250 percent more likely to be involved in an international conflict than other countries. So every time we fill up our gas tanks, we're adding fuel to those conflicts.

## —WHAT CAN WE DO ABOUT IT?—
# Get Moving!

**NO MATTER WHERE YOU TRAVEL,** you can think about the impact of how you get around and find options that work best for you and your family, your community, and the Earth.

Ride a bike. Bicycles can get you farther than walking, and a lot faster. If you get a rack with panniers or a basket, you can carry more. If you don't want to own a bike, considering joining a bike share.

Use public transportation. If your area has a public transit system, use it! Many cities offer a discounted pass for school-aged kids, which makes taking the bus or subway more affordable. And most transit systems have room for bicycles, so a combination of biking and public transit can get you a long way.

### WORLDWIDE WHEELS

Some organizations collect donated bicycles and ship them to countries where few people own their own cars, where public transport isn't an option, or where people live in remote villages. Owning a bike opens doors for those who would otherwise have to spend hours getting to school, work, or anywhere else.

## Back to School

Fewer kids get enough daily exercise than they did in the past. At the same time, more kids are obese or overweight, which can cause health problems such as diabetes. One simple way to get healthier is to walk, wheel, skateboard, or bike to school. If your school is too far away, drive or bus part of the way and walk the rest. Even a daily 15-minute walk or wheel helps.

Kids who walk to school tend to be in a better mood throughout the day and are more likely to stay awake in class. Some research suggests it can even improve your grades! It's also a great way to be independent and spend time with friends.

## Staycations

When we go somewhere new, we experience how other cultures live and think. If your family is planning a holiday, why not talk to your parents about ways to travel more responsibly?

You could look for low-impact experiences rather than luxury resorts or extravagant package deals. Can you drive or take the train instead of flying? Are you staying in a place that aims to lower its environmental footprint in any way? When you arrive, respect the local environment, whether that means taking public transit, staying on hiking trails, not feeding the animals in the wild, not littering, or reusing your towels.

You can also take a "staycation" or "holistay" in your own country or city. Staycations can be easier to plan, more affordable, and less stressful than an international holiday. And you might find something new and surprising in your own neighborhood.

Walking, biking, or low-impact vacations are easier on the environment *and* your finances. Keep reading to find out how less money is a good thing.

### ~LET'S BIKE!~

If you don't already have a bike, many communities have earn-a-bike programs. The first Earn-a-Bike program was started by Bikes Not Bombs in Boston, Massachusetts, in 1990. Since then, similar programs have been set up in communities across Canada and the United States. Through a combination of learning bike repair and volunteering, participants can earn their own set of wheels.

### MAKE the BIG CHANGE

### DON'T DRIVE!

More and more teens are choosing not to get their driver's license, or buy a car, even when they're legally old enough. Why not join the car-free movement?

# 8

# MONEY

## —WHAT'S THE ISSUE?—

## More Money, More Mess

•

**WHEN YOU THINK ABOUT MONEY,** what goes through your mind? Are you happy with how much you have? If you, like many of us, think that more money would solve all your problems, think again.

Let's say you buy whole, healthy food, bring reusable bags to the store, turn off your air-conditioning, and walk to school. These are all good things to do, for many reasons. You stand to be much healthier and happier. But your efforts to "save the planet" may not be helping as much as you might think. Why? Because your address can have a larger impact than your attitude.

## Money Speaks Louder Than Intentions

No matter how we live, those of us in wealthier countries use more resources and create more pollution than most people in low-income countries. The wealthiest 10 percent of the world's population produces half of Earth's fossil-fuel emissions, but suffer the least from the consequences of the pollution. The poorest half of the world's population produce only 10 percent of global emissions, but are the most vulnerable to the effects of pollution, extreme weather, or natural disasters. If we have extra money we tend to spend it on more stuff, bigger homes, fancy cars, or luxuries like travel. And these extras damage the well-being of the natural world.

## Sharing Is Caring

Wealth can also make us less empathetic and less connected with other people or with our own actions. For example, buying stuff online is convenient, but it's something we can do at home, alone. Also, by simply paying for our goods and services, we can easily forget about the people, animals, and environment on the other side of the transaction. And that's when a lot of mistreatment happens.

Researchers have found that as we grow richer, we become less compassionate. This might be because wealthier people can lose the ability to recognize the emotions of others or pay attention to others. As well, less affluent people are more likely to notice people who need help or feel it's important to take care of the vulnerable.

However, there are benefits to having less money. Sharing, trading, or bartering, rather than buying new stuff, can be a way to meet and connect with people in our community.

coltan

## Overgrown

While our planet has limits, our current economic system depends on limitless growth. And often the projects that make the most money can lead to destruction. One example is coltan, a mineral used in devices like computers and cellphones, which has contributed to wars in the Democratic Republic of the Congo, where it is mined.

If our appetite for resources (like coltan) continues to grow, then these resources will continue to make more profit for the banks, corporations, and the people who invest in them.

Limitless growth requires us to consume more and more resources. And as we learned in the first chapter, that's just not sustainable. At some point, the whole system could collapse.

## Putting Our Money Where Our Mouth Is

Money can be a tool for change or a weapon, depending on how we choose to use it. Every dollar we spend can either support our community, our Earth, and our beliefs, or can harm them. When we buy processed, packaged food, we're supporting the fossil-fuel industry and industrial farms that produce that food, along with the pollution these create. But by sharing, using our neighborhood library, or supporting small, local businesses, we can support the people in our own community.

Think about it. Where is your money going? How are you using it?

### THE HAVES AND THE HAVE-NOTS

Is it better to call people "rich" and "poor," or "high-income" and "low-income"? Does it make sense to talk about countries being "First World" and "Third World" or "developed" and "undeveloped"? Some people think "poor" is degrading, while others think "low-income" glosses over the harsh realities of living in poverty.

But whatever word you choose, remember that you're talking about real people. Be as specific as possible and make sure you understand what the word really means, and the facts about who you're talking about. Rich or poor, developed or undeveloped, we're all individuals who have a story to tell.

In Rio de Janeiro, Brazil, wealthy neighborhoods and slums, known as *favelas*, exist side by side.

# Voluntary Simplicity

**WHEN I WAS YOUNGER,** I wanted to be a millionaire. Money was my passion and a hobby. When I grew older I was pretty successful at business. Today I could certainly have a large house, a shiny car, and fancy things if I wanted them.

But I discovered that our financial system causes a lot of destruction. When I learned that my bank was using my money to invest in projects that destroyed the Earth I took my money out. When I learned that my investments and retirement fund were supporting cigarette and fossil-fuel companies I got rid of those investments.

I became aware of the huge gap between the wealthy and the poor—in my country and around the world. The top one percent of people own nearly half the world's wealth. I decided I didn't want to have so much while others had so little. This awareness led me to choose a life of voluntary simplicity. Some would say I live in poverty. In financial terms, they're right. But my life is far from poor. I have no debts, no monthly bills, no credit cards. I've chosen to support the Earth and my community instead of corporations and banks.

For a year, I lived in the Teeny Greeny. My entire home was smaller than the average-sized bedroom.

## Turning a Bad Deed Into Good Deeds

I really loved my bamboo bike. Of all my possessions, it was one of the most important. Then one night, someone stole it. My soul was crushed.

I really wanted it back, but I asked myself, "How can I turn this into something good?" I knew first-hand how horrible it felt to have a bike stolen. And I knew lots of kids have had their bikes stolen and

Rob lived in Florida in this simple 100-square-foot (9.3 m²) tiny house built mostly with secondhand materials.

can't afford to replace them. So I started a fundraiser to flip this misfortune upside down and do something positive for the people in my community.

I started looking for my bike right away. I talked to dozens of people on the streets and they were extremely helpful. Following one clue at a time, I finally tracked down my bike and the young man who stole it. Rather than acting in anger, I treated him with compassion and kindness and I gave him a hug.

One woman who helped me lived on the streets. When she heard about my fundraiser, she pulled $5 from her pocket and asked me to give it to the kids. I was blown away by her generosity.

So many people donated to this fundraiser that I was able to donate 50 bikes to kids who couldn't afford one. Many of them had had their own bike stolen.

This experience was a real adventure for me and an emotional journey. But it was also an incredibly positive experience. Together, with everyone's help and support, we turned one bad deed into dozens of good deeds.

This is just one example of how money can be used for good. Can you think of any other ways?

Before I left San Diego, I came up with another way to support my community: I auctioned off my tiny home. We raised $10,000 to build tiny homes for people without homes.

# Connecting Our Money to Our Values

**THERE'S A REASON ROB GIVES** so much to others. It feels good. It makes him happy. It changes his community for the better. So how can we use money to improve our planet and our community, and make ourselves happy?

A volunteer delivers tree seedlings—and smiles!—to students.

## Want What You Have . . .

And don't want what you don't have. The more time we spend appreciating what we've got, the less time we'll have to wish we had more. Which means we'll need to make less money. Our brain will be filled with more positive thoughts instead.

But it takes practice to actually see what we have. We're used to practicing our multiplication tables or catching a ball to perfect our skills, but we can improve our attitudes and mental skills with daily practice too. Practice gratitude by asking yourself what you're thankful for every day. If it's been a hard day, it might be something small, like good weather, or not missing the bus, or having a bed to sleep in. But chances are, you can think of *something*.

## Dig a Little Deeper

The way we spend our money says a lot about what's important to us and what we support. But how do we know what we're supporting? How would we know, for example, if our favorite clothing company uses child labor or produces their clothes in sweatshops? With a little research, we can learn a lot. Ask questions. Look for information from credible sources. Keep your mind open.

## MAKE the BIG CHANGE

### RADICAL GENEROSITY

Rob gives 100 percent of his media income to nonprofit organizations. How much could you give to others? Could you commit to giving away 10 percent of your allowance to a cause that matters to you?

## BUY NOTHING DAY

In November, try celebrating Buy Nothing Day—an international day of protest against consumerism. Do you think you could go for a full day without spending any money? But don't stop at one day. Could you spend nothing for a week? A month? What's your limit?

## Talk About It

Sometimes we're not even aware of what we value or believe. Talking to friends or adults can help us figure it out. You can even make it a game. Write down some Big Questions on pieces of paper. Put a few in a hat or bag, and then pull one out to start a conversation. Here are some examples:

- What would you do if you won the lottery?

- If your house was burning down, what would you save first?

- What would you do if you found a wallet on the sidewalk?

- Do some people deserve to be poor? Do some deserve to be rich?

- What would you do for $1,000? What would you never do, no matter how much you were paid?

- Is money the only reason to get a job? Are there other reasons?

**–KIDS HELPING KIDS–**

**WHEN VISHAL VIJAY AND HIS BROTHER ISHAN** traveled to northern India to visit family, they saw street children living in extreme poverty. The experience made a big impression on Vishal, who was 11 years old at the time. When he returned home to Oakville, Ontario, he and his brother and three friends started a group to fight for the rights of children in other countries. Today, their nonprofit organization, EveryChildNow, has clubs in schools across Canada.

We live in a society that sees us as consumers. Our stuff defines us. But it doesn't have to be this way. We can choose to value our accomplishments, relationships, or the natural world (or all three) instead and live with less. By disconnecting from our possessions, it's easier to connect to what's really important. How does that work? Keep reading to find out.

# 9

# CONNECTION

## —WHAT'S THE ISSUE?—

## Disconnection

•

YOU'VE PROBABLY HEARD PEOPLE SAY that humans are social animals. It's true. We need strong connections with family, friends, and neighbors to survive and thrive.

But despite this, we're getting out less and less. We tend to have fewer close friends now than we did 30 years ago. According to one study, three out of every five Americans say they feel lonely. Similar surveys in Canada, the United Kingdom, and Australia discovered that an alarming number of people feel lonely. In 2018, the UK government appointed a government minister of loneliness to tackle this "sad reality of modern life."

## The Price of Loneliness

Without close friends, we're more likely to feel lonely, depressed, or anxious. In severe cases, this leads to suicidal or violent thoughts or actions. Our body perceives isolation as a threat and releases stress hormones to protect us. But if we experience the stress of loneliness for a long time, it can affect our physical health as much as our mental state. When we're chronically lonely and depressed, we become more vulnerable to almost every disease that has been studied.

When we make connections in our communities—in our neighborhood or school or even virtual communities—we feel less lonely. We're less likely to feel depressed and more likely to recover from stressful situations.

## What's Changed?

There are many reasons why we're more likely to feel lonely and depressed these days. Overly busy schedules. Worry about environmental crises. A tense political climate. Racism and hate crimes, which make some of us less likely to be friendly to neighbors or strangers. Maybe it feels easier to stay home and keep to ourselves.

We also tend to feel down when we spend less time outside in nature, or exercise less, or eat less healthy food.

## Are Screens and Devices Bad?

Some people believe that spending more time on electronic devices leads to isolation and depression. And since 2007, when the iPhone was first released, rates of depression in teens have steadily increased. Since then, teens have reported that they are less likely to go out or date and more likely to feel depressed.

When teens do go out, they are more likely to record and broadcast the event on social media. Have you ever looked at posts with photos of your friends hanging out and felt like you were the only one who wasn't invited?

But do iPhones actually cause depression, or are teens depressed for other reasons and just happen to have iPhones too? It's hard to say. And our devices also help us at school, at work, or to stay in touch with friends and family. It's a contradiction: these devices keep us connected but they can also disconnect us from our closest friends and loved ones.

Electronic devices, social media platforms, and things with screens are merely tools, like a hammer is a tool. You can use these tools to create something useful or beautiful, or you can use them to harm and destroy. We need to use these tools wisely.

How can we stay connected with our family, friends, and community? How can we use these powerful tools to improve our lives? How can we use them with intention, rather than letting them take over our lives?

### WHAT DO WE REALLY NEED?

Forget money, stuff, and fame. We're more likely to be healthy and happy when we feel loved and that we belong. Scientists agree: our bodies need air and nourishment and movement to simply stay alive, but without social connection, we're unlikely to thrive. Our basic needs are:

1. Food

2. Water

3. Shelter

4. Sleep

5. Other people to connect with

6. New things and experiences

# Disconnected to Connect

**IT'S HARD TO ADMIT THIS,** but I often can't stop checking my computer and online devices, even when I don't want to. I tell myself I'll just quickly check my email and, hours later, I'm still online. I stay up too late because I'm online, or I go straight to my computer as soon as I wake up.

I remember biking across the country during my Off the Grid adventure. I would pull off the road to read comments on my social media posts or constantly check my email. I was still glued to my cellphone, even when I was surrounded by all the beauty in the world!

My last relationship suffered because I often felt it was more important to be on the computer than to spend quality time with the one I loved.

## Taking Control

I started to wonder if I had an addiction. Through some research I found that I had an "extremely habitual pattern" but not quite an addiction. When I'm away from my devices, I don't experience withdrawal. If my devices aren't around, I don't miss them. I feel better. But if they're around, I can't resist them.

When I woke up to my problem, I decided to take control of my situation. I needed to get my life into balance. I embarked on an extreme adventure of disconnection to reconnect with what matters. I bought a one-way ticket to Panama and landed 4,000 miles (6,400 km) and seven countries away from home with just the clothes on my back and my passport. No phone (I left it at home), no computer, and no money. I wanted to get home by meeting real people and connecting with them in a deep way. Could I get there by relying only on the goodness of others and my own real-life skills?

Projects such as planting Community Fruit Trees keep me connected to others.

## Share My Way Home

What could possibly go wrong?

I experienced days with little or no food and nights with nowhere to stay. I hitchhiked in extreme weather, out in the middle of nowhere. There were times when I honestly didn't know if I would make it.

But when you travel with no money or technology, it forces you out of your comfort zone; it takes you to places and introduces you to people that you never would have seen or met in any other way.

Through these travels I've found that people with less are often happier than my friends who have more. Maybe they value their relationships more. Or they are more connected to their community. They might have one TV and gather around it together, rather than each sitting in their own rooms with their own screen. Or more likely, rather than watching soccer or playing a soccer video game, the kids are outside actually playing soccer.

I used social media to help connect with other changemakers on several occasions, like here in Paris at our Plastic Attack demonstration.

## An Eye-Opening Experience

That trip helped me to understand something important: we will take care of each other when we actually need each other. Without a smartphone in my pocket, I needed *people* to help me get home. Since then, I've learned to be more aware of how and when I use devices.

I use social media as a tool to create positive change. I use email to connect with friends and for my environmental projects. I talk about prioritizing health and happiness and connecting to nature, and try hard to do so, but my devices often get in the way. My goal is to drastically decrease my level of hypocrisy and be open and honest with myself and others.

# Create Community

**ROB TRAVELED FAR AWAY TO** find connection and community, but you can find it right outside your front door.

Connecting with your family, friends, community, or culture reminds you that you are important and that you belong.

## Live in the Real World

The first step to strengthening your community might be to turn off your phone. But if you have trouble ignoring your device, give yourself limits. Put it away an hour before you go to bed, so that you can wind down before sleep. Get into the habit of waiting at least half an hour before you check it in the morning. Lock it in a cupboard if you have to, or ask someone you trust to safeguard it for you.

How can you make it *less* convenient to check your social media? Create barriers to help you resist the urge. Leave your phone in your backpack when you're visiting a friend, so you can give them your full attention. Or turn off all notifications so you aren't reminded of your device every time a message or comment comes in.

Try some digital spring cleaning—unfollow any connection you aren't genuinely interested in, or unfriend people and unfollow pages that post negative messages. Delete all apps that aren't necessary or helpful.

And when you are on social media, remember to be respectful with every single message you put out there—not just with your own posts but with every "like," emoji, or comment. Aim to be the friendly face at the digital party, not the bully.

## Find a Safe Place

It can be hard to find a safe place to meet others. Ask an adult you trust to help you. Local libraries often offer after-school programs for free, or check out what's happening at your community center. Are there any teams or school clubs you could join?

### *In Your Neighborhood*

- Take a walk around your neighborhood (bring a friend or an adult if you don't want to go alone). Say hello to your neighbors.

- Consider starting or helping out at a community garden or local farm.

- Try dog walking, babysitting, delivering the newspaper, or yard cleaning—you'll meet people while you do it.

### *At Your School*

- Join a club to find people who share the same interests as you. What's your passion? If you can't find a club or team, consider starting one yourself.

### —TEEN GREEN TEAM—

**BK ROT,** a composting service in Brooklyn, New York, transforms waste into a quality product that both serves the community and gives back to the Earth. Staffed by young people of color, the project's collectors haul organic waste by bicycle. Composters then process the waste, bag it, and sell it locally. Though their facility is small, they are able to process up to 15,000 pounds (6,800 kg) of food waste a month. The BK ROT team emphasizes creating community, a local green economy, and a space for the environmental and climate justice leaders of the future.

Strong relationships, in your school or neighborhood, aren't made overnight. But once you create those connections with friends, loved ones, and your community, your support network will be wider and stronger.

# —CONCLUSION—
# You Matter! Yes, You!

**OVER THE YEARS MANY PEOPLE** have asked me,
"But Rob, is it really worth trying? I'm just one in 7 billion.
Can I really make a difference?"

My answer is an absolute YES!

I answer *yes* because I believe that life matters. I believe you matter. I believe the life of every animal and plant species matters. Through our daily actions we can live in a way that harms others, or in a way that increases the quality of life of others.

Community garden projects are a great way to create positive change and connect with others.

Now, don't feel like all of the world's problems are your fault. And you shouldn't feel responsible for solving them all. In fact, I don't think you or I or any one person can "save the world." No single person can clean up all the garbage in the ocean, but you can work with your friends to clean up your local beach or river. No single person can eliminate world hunger. But you can volunteer at a food bank or grow a garden and share the harvest with a neighbor who doesn't have access to healthy food. Your actions won't change the whole world, but you can brighten one person's day or leave one beach cleaner.

The small changes we make as individuals matter greatly, but they won't change the entire system. The system is too huge for anyone to change single-handedly. But at the same time, the system is made up of people like you and me. As you make these small changes, you'll feel stronger and better able to stand up for the Earth, for cleaner communities, for other species. And as more of us change, the system itself changes. Corporations and government are just as (or more) responsible for creating the problems, *and* for solving them. They're also made up of individual people like you and me. And they must change too.

## FREE TO BE ME

If I could go back and visit myself when I was your age and give myself just one piece of advice, I know exactly what I would say: "Don't worry so much about what others think!" I would tell my 12-year-old self, "Our 'normal' lives are actually destroying what you love." When I embraced these ideas, once I was an adult, I felt free and strong enough to complete the difficult journeys that you've read about in this book. And once you free yourself from what society expects and thinks is "normal," and you live instead according to your beliefs and ethics, you too can accomplish your own amazing adventures. Start your journey toward a more sustainable life with one small step and then some big leaps!

Think of the wonders humans can accomplish when we work together. Even if each individual person seems to be doing something small—like buying less, or eating food from local farms, or reducing the waste they produce—together we can create something huge.

My hope is that after reading this book, you feel empowered to go out and do one small thing, and then another and another and another until you become the change you wish to see in the world.

# —GLOSSARY—

**biofuel:** a source of energy that is made directly from living matter (such as plants) using modern processes. Three examples of biofuels are ethanol (often made from corn), biodiesel (made from vegetable oils and liquid animal fats), and biogas (which is methane from animal manure and other organic material). In contrast, while fossil fuels (such as oil) are also made from living matter, it takes millions of years for them to be produced.

**biomass:** organic matter that is used as a source of energy. Some examples of biomass are wood, waste from food crops (such as wheat straw or corn husks), or manure.

**carbon footprint:** the amount of carbon dioxide and other carbon compounds (greenhouse gases) that are produced when fossil fuels are consumed by an activity or to produce, transport, store, or dispose of something. Carbon footprints are one way for scientists and researchers to calculate how a product, person, or action affects the environment. See also *land footprint* and *water footprint*.

**climate change:** a change in historical or predictable climate patterns in a certain region or across the globe. This term is used to describe the changes that have occurred since the mid- to late 1900s, which are largely due to the higher levels of greenhouse gases in the atmosphere.

**extreme weather event:** severe, unexpected, unusual, or unseasonal weather, such as snow, rain, drought, flood, or a storm that is rare for the place where it occurs.

**fossil fuel:** a fuel, such as coal, oil, or gas, that was formed over millions of years from the remains of dead plants and animals or other natural resources.

**greenhouse gas (GHG):** a gas that traps the sun's heat in Earth's atmosphere and radiates it back to Earth's surface. Greenhouse gases include carbon dioxide, methane, and nitrous oxide and are often produced when fossil fuels are burned.

**greywater:** water that has been used (for example, from baths, sinks, or washing machines) and is then used again for another purpose (such as for watering plants). By contrast, sewage (or blackwater) is water that must be filtered and treated before reuse.

**land footprint:** the total amount of land needed to produce a product or used by an organization or country.

**minimalism:** when describing a lifestyle, it means living with fewer possessions or with extreme simplicity.

**nonrenewable energy:** energy that is produced from sources that are natural but that can't be replenished as quickly as they are consumed. Fossil fuels such as oil, natural gas, and coal are examples of nonrenewable energy resources. While fossil fuels can be renewed, the process takes millions of years.

**poverty line (or poverty level):** countries or governments estimate the minimal income for a person or family to meet their basic needs. If a person or family live off less than this amount, then they are living below the poverty line.

**renewable energy:** energy that is produced from sources that are naturally replenished. Common examples include energy produced

from wind, solar, geothermal heat, water, and some biomass.

**tiny home:** a new style in architecture that supports living simply in small homes. Generally, a house that is 400 square feet (37 m²) or smaller is considered a tiny home—smaller than a two-car garage, which is about 575–725 square feet, (53–67 m²).

**water footprint:** the total amount of fresh water consumed (evaporated) and/or polluted to produce and deliver a product or service.

# —RESOURCES—

## Books, Reports, and Videos

Ayer, Paula. *Foodprints: The Story of What We Eat*. Toronto: Annick Press, 2015.

Baehr, Birke. "What's Wrong With Our Food System." Filmed August 2010, Asheville, NC, TED video, 4:58, ted.com/talks/birke_baehr_what_s_wrong_with_our_food_system?.

Banyard, Antonia, and Paula Ayer. *Eat Up! An Info-graphic Exploration of Food*. Toronto: Annick Press, 2017.

––. *Water Wow! An Infographic Exploration*. Toronto: Annick Press, 2016.

Biggs, Emma, and Steven Biggs. *Gardening With Emma: Grow and Have Fun*. North Adams, MA: Storey Publishing, 2019.

Greenfield, Rob. *Zero-Waste Kids: Hands-On Projects and Activities to Reduce, Reuse, and Recycle*. Beverly, MA: Quarry Books, 2022.

Jones, Kari. *A Fair Deal: Shopping for Social Justice*. Victoria: Orca Book Publishers, 2017.

Leonard, Annie. *The Story of Stuff: How Our Obsession With Stuff Is Trashing the Planet, Our Communities and Our Health—And a Vision for Change*. New York: Free Press, 2010.

Mulder, Michelle. *Brilliant! Shining a Light on Sustainable Energy*. Victoria: Orca Book Publishers, 2013.

Nikkel, Lori, et al. *The Avoidable Crisis of Food Waste: The Roadmap*. Toronto: Second Harvest and Value Chain Management International, 2019.

Pêgo, Ana, and Isabel Minhós Martins. *Plasticus Maritimus: An Invasive Species*. Vancouver: Greystone Kids, 2020.

Tate, Nikki. *Better Together: Creating Community in an Uncertain World*. Victoria: Orca Book Publishers, 2018.

## Websites

**Autumn Peltier:** facebook.com/Waterwarrior1/
**BK ROT:** bkrot.org
**Donate Don't Dump:** donatedontdump.org
**Ecological Footprints and Earth Overshoot Day:** overshootday.org
**EveryChildNow:** everychildnow.mystrikingly.com
**FareShare (UK):** fareshare.org.uk
**Global FoodBanking Network:** foodbanking.org/what-we-do/our-global-reach/
**K–12 Food Rescue (USA):** foodrescue.net
**Little Free Library:** littlefreelibrary.org
**OzHarvest (Australia):** ozharvest.org
**Rob Greenfield:** robgreenfield.org
**Second Harvest (Canada):** secondharvest.ca
**The Story of Stuff Project:** storyofstuff.org
**Water Footprint Calculator (plus more information about water use):** watercalculator.org/
**Zero Waste Family:** zerowastefamily.com
**ZooShare:** zooshare.ca

# —SELECTED SOURCES—

Baumeister, R.F., and M.R. Leary. "The Need to Belong: Desire for Interpersonal Attachments as a Fundamental Human Motivation," *Psychological Bulletin* 117, no. 3 (May 1995): 497–529. pubmed.ncbi.nlm.nih.gov/7777651.

Clift, Jon, and Amanda Cuthbert. *Water: Use Less—Save More*. Devon, UK: Green Books, 2006.

Colgan, Jeff D. *Petro-Aggression: When Oil Causes War*. Cambridge, MA: Cambridge University Press, 2013.

Gerber, P.J., et al. *Tackling Climate Change Through Livestock: A Global Assessment of Emissions and Mitigation Opportunities*. Rome: FAO, 2013. fao.org/news/story/en/item/197623/icode.

Glendenning, Lauren. "Social Isolation and Loneliness: A Talk About Coronavirus's Effects on Mental Health," *Post Independent*, April 23, 2020. postindependent.com/news/social-isolation-and-loneliness-a-talk-about-coronaviruss-effects-on-mental-health-sponsored.

Gravagna, Nicole. "Six Fundamental Human Needs We Need to Meet to Live Our Best Lives," *Forbes*, February 5, 2018. forbes.com/sites/quora/2018/02/05/six-fundamental-human-needs-we-need-to-meet-to-live-our-best-lives/#64e3b288344a.

Grewal, Daisy. "How Wealth Reduces Compassion," *Scientific American*, April 10, 2012. scientificamerican.com/article/how-wealth-reduces-compassion.

Gustavsson, Jenn, et al. *Global Food Losses and Food Waste: Extent, Causes and Prevention*. Rome: FAO, 2011. fao.org/3/i2697e/i2697e.pdf.

Hawken, Peter, ed. *Drawdown: The Most Comprehensive Plan Ever Proposed to Reverse Global Warming*. New York: Penguin, 2017.

Hill, Jacob. "The Environmental Impact of Roads," EnvironmentalScience.org, n.d. environmentalscience.org/roads.

Kaza, Silpa, et al. *What a Waste 2.0: A Global Snapshot of Solid Waste Management to 2050*. Washington, DC: World Bank, 2018. openknowledge.worldbank.org/handle/10986/30317.

Kim, Janice J., et al. "Traffic-Related Air Pollution Near Busy Roads: The East Bay Children's Respiratory Health Study," *American Journal of Respiratory and Critical Care Medicine* 170, no. 5 (2004). doi.org/10.1164/rccm.200403-281OC.

· · · · · · · · · · · · · · · · · · · · · · · · · · · · · · · · · · · · · · · ·

**Note to readers:**

The statistics and sources in this book are drawn from the latest information available at the time of writing. In cases where numbers may vary, averages have been used. Some figures have been rounded up or down for the sake of simplicity. Unless otherwise noted, online sources were last consulted in June 2020.

Kraus, Michael W., Stéphane Côté, and Dacher Keltner. "Social Class, Contextualism, and Empathic Accuracy," *Psychological Science* 21, no. 11 (November 2010): 1716–23. doi.org/10.1177/0956797610387613.

Leahy, Stephen. *Your Water Footprint: The Shocking Facts About How Much Water We Use to Make Everyday Products.* Toronto: Firefly Books, 2014.

Leonard, Annie. *The Story of Stuff: How Our Obsession With Stuff Is Trashing the Planet, Our Communities and Our Health—And a Vision for Change.* New York: Free Press, 2010.

Lim, Michelle H., Robert Eres, and Claire Peck. *The Young Australian Loneliness Survey: Understanding Loneliness in Adolescence and Young Adulthood,* Iverson Health Innovation Research Institute & Centre for Mental Health, Swinburne University of Technology, 2019. vichealth.vic.gov.au/loneliness-survey.

Lutsey, Nicholas P., and Dan Sperling. "Transportation and Greenhouse Gas Mitigation," UC Davis: Institute of Transportation Studies, 2008. escholarship.org/uc/item/6fz1z05g.

Naik, S.N., et al. "Production of First and Second Generation Biofuels: A Comprehensive Review," *Renewable and Sustainable Energy Reviews* 14, no. 2 (February 2010): 578–97. doi.org/10.1016/j.rser.2009.10.003.

Nikkel, Lori, et al. *The Avoidable Crisis of Food Waste: Technical Report.* Toronto: Second Harvest and Value Chain Management International, 2019. secondharvest.ca/wp-content/uploads/2019/01/Avoidable-Crisis-of-Food-Waste-Technical-Report-January-17-2019.pdf.

Schor, Juliet B. *Born to Buy: The Commercialized Child and the New Consumer Culture.* New York: Scribner, 2004.

Syme, S. Leonard, and Miranda L. Ritterman. "The Importance of Community Development for Health and Well-Being," *Community Development Investment Review* 3 (January 2009): 1–13. frbsf.org/community-development/files/syme_ritterman.pdf.

# —IMAGE CREDITS—

**Front cover** girl © tirc83/iStockphoto.com; Rob with Abhishek Shastri, courtesy of Pallavi Shastri;
boy © Waridsara_HappyChildren/Shutterstock.com; landfill © vchal/Shutterstock.com; **ii** photos submitted by
changemakers, from left to right, courtesy of: (beach cleanup) The Future Kids; (home garden) Sandy Haynes;
(conserving water and pushing water buckets) Cameron and Alicia Gasaway; (backyard gardeners) Ana Lopez;
(tree planters) Bonnie Toye; (garbage cleanup) Cassandra Pugh; (orangutan pledge) Jack aka Kid Conservationist;
**iii** more submitted photos, from left to right, courtesy of: (building with repurposed pallets) Marcus Chapman;
(climate striker) Harvey Hennessy; (college gardener) Sara Beadle; (vertical tower garden) Pinar Ozyetis; (perma-
culture group in Bali) Amal Elbahnasawy; (urban gardener) Boris Lennaertz; (container gardener) Pauline Mwangi;
**iv** Rob in garden by Sierra Ford Photography; **1** landfill © vchal/Shutterstock.com; **2–3** Rob in front of house, and
Rob eating collards by Sierra Ford Photography; **4–5** garage © Boogich/iStockphoto.com; **6** teen in bedroom
© denozy/iStockphoto.com; **7** cats shaunl/iStockphoto.com; **9** Rob with 44 possessions © Ornella; **10** paintbrushes
© harmpeti/iStockphoto.com; Little Free Library © KenWiedemann/iStockphoto.com; **11** Isabella Syren, courtesy
of The Zero Waste Family; **12–13** landfill aerial photo © AvigatorPhotographer/iStockphoto.com; **14** city landfill
© Ralph125/iStockphoto.com; flies © tzara/iStockphoto.com; banana peel © KaselowGraphics/iStockphoto.com;
cans © subjug/iStockphoto.com; **15** garbage bag © Michael Burrell/iStockphoto.com; **16** Rob on subway by Gary
Bencheghib; **17** Rob with Nancy Judd by Gary Bencheghib; Everett Sjolseth, courtesy of Sheila Sjolseth; Rob in New
York school, courtesy of Pallavi Shastri; Rob and boy in New York by Gary Bencheghib; **18** Future Kids after beach
cleanup, courtesy of The Future Kids; water bottle © Kidsada Manchinda/Shutterstock.com; **19** gift in
furoshiki wrap © piotrmilewski/iStockphoto.com; Rob with Abhishek Shastri, courtesy of Pallavi Shastri; **20–21** wasted
produce © joerngebhardt68/Shutterstock.com; **22** vegetables in landfill © Joaquin Corbalan/iStockphoto.com;
crate of apples © K_Thalhofer/iStockphoto.com; **23** buffet © Maryviolet/iStockphoto.com; restaurant leftovers
© EXTREME-PHOTOGRAPHER/iStockphoto.com; peppers on conveyor belt © jeffbergen/iStockphoto.com; grocery
store shopper © VLG/iStockphoto.com; paper bag © mustafa güner/iStockphoto.com; **24** Rob in dumpster by
Sierra Ford Photography; **26** soup © fcafotodigital/iStockphoto.com; **27** school cafeteria, courtesy of K–12 Food
Rescue; Gabrielle Posard and volunteers, courtesy of Donate Don't Dump; **28–29** beef cattle in feedlots © Bim/
iStockphoto.com; **30** industrial chicken farm © Henadzi Pechan/iStockphoto.com; potato chips © clubfoot/
iStockphoto.com; **31** bread on assembly line © sergeyryzhov/iStockphoto.com, corn in field © stoonn/iStockphoto.com;
**32** Rob in outdoor kitchen and green smoothie by Sierra Ford Photography; **33** planting community trees, and sweet
potatoes, and beekeeping, by Live Wonderful Photography; **34** home baking © RichLegg/iStockphoto.com;
foraging garlic leaves, courtesy of Natasha Carrington; **35** community garden © SolStock/iStockphoto.com;
Seed Library courtesy of Alicia Serratos; **36–37** hosing down sidewalk © photosaint/iStockphoto.com;
**38** garden hose © Tharin Sinlapachai/Shutterstock.com; electrical outlet © EHStock/iStockphoto.com;
**39** hamburger ©Kuzmik_A/iStockphoto.com; tomatoes © anna1311/iStockphoto.com; T-shirt © airdone/
iStockphoto.com; chocolate bar © robtek/iStockphoto.com; fried egg © Pineapple Studio/iStockphoto.com;

# —INDEX—

AN INDEX IS an alphabetized list of key words that appear in the text. You can use the index by looking for a subject that interests you, like "composting" or "greenhouse gases" or "nuclear energy." The numbers after each key word are the page numbers where you will find information. Page numbers in a range (for example, 6–7) tell you that information is found on pages 6 *and* 7.

A key word might lead you to more specific subjects. So, if you look up "food" you'll also discover the page number where you can read about "growing your own." Sometimes you might think of a key word but the information will actually be under a different word, so the index will suggest "*See*" (for example: "garbage. *See* waste"). Or maybe there's more information listed under another key word, so the index will suggest "*See also*" (for example: "health. *See also* diet").

It's fun to take a quick look at the index. You might find something surprising like… "zoo poo"?

air travel, 54; and the impact on the environment, 54

animals: dangers to, 55; on farms, 30–1, 42

Anishinabek First Nation, 43

Australia: and food waste, 20, 22; and loneliness, 68; and waste production, 14

bicycles. *See* cycling

Bikes Not Bombs, 59

biofuels, 47; biogas from zoo poo, 51; how they damage the environment, 47

BK ROT, 75

Brazil, 63

Buy Nothing Day, 67

Canada, 23, 54, 59; and food waste, 20, 22; and loneliness, 68; and waste production, 14; and water use, 38

cars, 3, 8, 52, 54–5, 59; advantages and disadvantages, 56; going car-free, 59; how they affect our communities, 54–5; how they pollute the air, 54; how they threaten wildlife, 55; what they cost, 54, 56

China, 7

clothing, 10, 11, 66; and water-wise washing, 38, 42

coal, 46; how it pollutes, 46; how it's mined, 46

community gardens/fruit trees, 33, 34, 72, 75, 76

composting, 14, 19, 26, 34, 41, 75

connecting with others, 68–75; how to create community, 74–5; and our screens and devices, 71–5; at school, 75; why it's important, 68, 70, 74. *See also* loneliness

cycling, 24–5, 40, 48, 55, 56–8, 59, 64–5; donating and sharing bikes, 58; Earn-a-Bike programs, 59

Democratic Republic of the Congo, 63

diet, 3, 31, 34, 42; cooking from scratch, 34; energy-conscious eating, 51; how it affects our health, 17, 30–1, 32, 34–5, 70; how to eat in a "planet-friendly" way, 34–5

Donate Don't Dump, 27

donating: bicycles, 58, 65; clothing, 10; food, 27; money 66; stuff, 8, 10–11

dumpster diving, 20, 24–5, 26, 32

Earn-a-Bike programs, 59

electricity, 7, 15, 46, 47, 49, 50; from fossil fuels, 46, 49, 50; from nuclear energy, 47; from renewable sources, 46, 47, 49; how much we use, 49–50; what it's used for, 7, 15, 31, 39

energy, 45–51; how much we use, 49, 50; renewable and nonrenewable, 46, 47, 50; where it comes from, 46–7. *See also* electricity; fossil fuels; nuclear energy

environmental damage: from energy production, 46–7; from industrial farming, 30, 31; from pollution, 7, 15, 30, 31, 39, 46–7; from transportation, 54–6; from wasting resources, 7

EveryChildNow, 67

5 Gyres, 19

food: buying locally grown, 35, 51, 77; foraging for, 32–3, 34; growing your own, 11, 26, 32–3, 35, 43, 76; natural/organic, 35; reasons to avoid processed food, 17, 30–1, 32, 35, 63. *See also* diet; food system

food packaging, 31; going package-free, 19, 63; where it ends up, 16, 31

food system, 29–35; how commercial farms operate, 30, 63; how much energy food production uses, 31; why topsoil is important, 30

food waste, 14, 19, 20–7, 32, 34, 75; in dumpsters, 24–7; at home, 26; how much is wasted, 17, 20–2, 27; how waste affects the environment, 23; in schools, 23, 27; in stores, 26–7; why it's wasted, 22–3, 26

forests: damage caused by clearing, 7, 23, 30, 47; pollution of, 7, 15

fossil fuels, 46, 47, 62; how they release greenhouse gases, 31, 46–7; what it costs to use them, 46, 51; what they're used for, 7, 15, 23, 30, 31, 39, 46, 47, 49, 63. See also coal; gas; oil

fracking. See hydraulic fracturing

Future Kids club, 18

Gandhi, Mahatma, 3

garbage. See waste

gas, 31, 39, 46, 47, 56, 57; how it pollutes, 31, 54

gratitude, 66

greenhouse gases (GHGs), 15, 31, 46–7; and climate change, 15, 31; created by transportation, 54

greywater, uses for, 40, 41, 42–3

health: and exposure to toxic chemicals and pollution, 30, 51; looking after your emotional/mental health, 3, 7, 9, 70–1; looking after your physical health, 3, 30–1, 33–5, 54, 58, 61, 70–1. See also diet

hoarding and collecting, 7–8

housing: bigger homes for more stuff, 6; smaller living spaces, 8, 64–5

humanure, 41

hydraulic fracturing ("fracking"), 47; how it pollutes, 47

India, 7, 67

Judd, Nancy, 17

K–12 Food Rescue, 27

landfill, 8, 15–16, 26, 31; food packaging in, 31

Little Free Libraries, 10

loneliness, 68, 70; how it affects us physically and mentally, 70; why we feel lonely, 70

mining, 47; energy used by, 31, 47; for coltan, 63; pollution created by, 46; waste from, 15

money, 61–7; connecting it to your values, 64, 66–7; donating it, 66; and feeling connected to others, 62; how wealth is linked to use of resources, 62; and voluntary simplicity, 64; what money can (and can't) do, 61, 62, 63, 73

nuclear energy, 46, 47; and radioactive waste, 47

oil, 47; and oil spills, 2–3, 47, 56; and oil wars, 56, 57

Panama, 72

Peltier, Autumn, 43

phones. See smartphones and devices

plastic: in our waste, 14, 15; in our waterways, 15, 31; pollution from, 19

pollution, 2–3, 7, 15, 39, 47, 62; from energy production, 46–7, 51; from industrial farms, 30, 63; from plastic, 15, 19, 31; from transportation, 54–6; how it damages our health, 51, 54; in our waterways, 30, 31, 39, 46–7

Posard, Gabrielle, 27

public transportation, 55, 58, 59; what it costs, 58

raw materials. See resources/raw materials

recycling, 8, 15, 16, 18, 19; how it uses energy, 15

reducing, 18; giving waste-free gifts, 19

Repair Cafés, 19

resources/raw materials, 7, 14, 62–3; forests and logging, 7, 23, 30, 47; how much we consume, 7, 62–3; mining, 7, 15, 31, 46–7

reusing, 18, 19; how to reuse water, 40, 42, 43

seed packs and seed libraries, 33, 35

Serratos, Alicia, 35; 3 Sisters Seed Box, 35

sharing instead of buying, 11, 62, 63, 73, 76; books, 10; cars and bikes, 56, 58; clothing, 10; food, 32, 33, 34, 76; seeds, 33, 35

Shastri, Abhishek, 19

Sjolseth, Everett, 17

smartphones and devices, 9, 74; and digital spring cleaning, 74; how they affect our connection to others, 71, 72, 73–4

social media, 71, 72, 74; positive uses for, 73

solar energy, 48–9, 57

South Africa, 18

Story of Stuff, The, 8

stuff, 4–11; buying less, 11, 77; how making it generates waste, 15; how much we have, 6; how to get rid of it, 7–11. See also hoarding and collecting; sharing instead of buying

Syren, Isabella, 11

Teeny Greeny house, 40, 64–5

toilets: composting, 41; how they waste water, 41, 42; water-efficient, 43

Toronto Zoo, 51

transportation, 50, 52–9; and greenhouse gas emissions, 54; how much energy it uses, 55; what it costs, 54, 56, 58, 59. See also air travel; cars; cycling; public transportation; walking

trash. See waste

"trash suit," 16–17

travel, 8, 10, 72–3; and staycations, 59; and your environmental footprint, 59

United Kingdom, 6; and food waste, 20, 22; and loneliness, 68; and waste production, 14

United States, 14, 23, 24–5, 27, 35, 40, 48, 54, 55, 57, 59; and food waste, 20, 22; and loneliness, 68; and waste production, 14; and water use, 38, 40

values: discovering yours, 67; linking values to spending, 64, 66–7

Vijay, Ishan, 67

Vijay, Vishal, 67

voluntary simplicity, 64

walking, 55, 58, 59, 75; benefits of, 58

waste, 13–19, 51, 57; how much we make, 13–14, 17; what we can do about it, 16–19, 77; what we throw away, 14–15; where it comes from, 15, 16, 18, 19; where it ends up, 15. See also food waste; landfill; water waste

water, 36–43; how much we need to survive, 36; how much we use in a day, 38; resources used to deliver it to us, 39, 50; using water to create energy, 38; using water to grow, make, move things, 38–9. See also greywater, uses for; pollution; water waste

water waste, 36–43; and laundry, 38, 42; and running the faucet, 38, 42, 50; and showers, 38, 40–1, 42, 43; and toilet flushing, 38, 41, 42, 43; using rainwater, 40; and watering lawns, 38, 43

waterways: plastic in, 15, 31; pollution of, 31, 39, 47, 76; used for hydroelectricity, 47

zoo poo, 51

# —ACKNOWLEDGMENTS—

**WE ARE CONTINUALLY INSPIRED BY** the children and youth who are making positive changes every day. To everyone who submitted photos, thank you for your creative thinking, enthusiasm, and generosity of spirit. Without the forward-thinking team at Greystone Kids, this book would never have happened, and we are truly grateful. Our insightful editor, Linda Pruessen, saw what was missing, fixed what was muddled, and trimmed the excess. The talented Belle Wuthrich made us look good, and our superb proofreader, Alison Strobel, caught our mistakes. Any remaining errors are our own. Huge thanks for making this a better book.

# —ABOUT THE AUTHORS—

**ROB GREENFIELD** is an activist and humanitarian dedicated to leading the way to a more sustainable and just world. He embarks on extreme projects to bring attention to important global issues and inspire positive change. His work has been covered by media worldwide, including *National Geographic*, and he's been named "the Robin Hood of modern times" by France 2 TV. Rob's life is an embodiment of Gandhi's philosophy to be the change he wishes to see in the world. He believes that our actions really do matter and that as individuals and communities we have the power to improve the world around us. Rob donates 100 percent of his media income to grassroots nonprofits and has committed to living simply and responsibly for life. Learn more at robgreenfield.org.

**ANTONIA BANYARD** writes for readers young and old. *Be the Change* is her sixth book for children. She loves writing, low-impact living, southern Africa, and being outdoors with her family. She emigrated from Zambia to Canada as a child and now lives in British Columbia.

All of Rob Greenfield's proceeds from the sale of this book will be donated to Indigenous women–led environmental organizations. For more information, visit robgreenfield.org/equity. A portion of Antonia Banyard's proceeds will be donated to Malambo Grassroots and other nonprofits that support environmental and social causes. See malambograssroots.ca and antoniabanyard.ca for details.

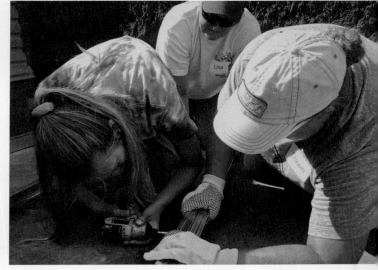